"Once again Colin Shaw shows us the future. As with *Building Great Customer Experiences* and *Revolutionize Your Customer Experience*, *The DNA of Customer Experience* develops and grows our knowledge of Customer Experience management further and at the same time introduces a practical and revolutionary technique to get value from it." – **Simon Fox**, *Chief Executive, HMV Group plc*

"The Customer Experience revolution continues as Colin Shaw with his new book again pushes the boundaries of our understanding. Using case studies and leading business research, Colin demonstrates the true value of emotions against the bottom line. This book pulls no punches. It tells you how much you can lose or gain in revenue by evoking the right emotions in your customers." – **Stuart Roberts**, *Customer Services Director, Barclaycard*

"Thought leadership at its best. *The DNA of Customer Experience* gets to the real heart of what it is that makes Customer Experience management so valuable as a means to increased profitability and differentiation in the over-commoditized world we live in today." – **Rhonda Dishongh**, *CRM Director, Memorial Hermann Hospital System*

"Truly excellent thought leadership. This book builds on the previous two and deals directly with the core issue that many executives struggle with, 'Intuitively I believe it but how can I make a compelling business case to convince others and justify the investment?' Essential reading for all those committed to creating great customer experiences in their organisations." – **Gary Price**, *Director of Customer Experience Implementation, Norwich Union*

"How many of us thought that life was just about price and product? Well after reading this book you'll all be wondering why you ever thought these were the only things. As surely as mariners came back from their ventures and said the earth is not flat, you will come away from this enthused and surprised by the true power of emotions." – **Liam Lambert**, *Operations Director, Europe, Mandarin Oriental*

"Truly enlightening, you will never think of the Customer Experience in the same way again." – **Darren Cornish**, *Head of Customer Experience, Norwich Union*

"Do you think your customers just make decisions rationally without consideration of their emotions? Well think again. In this new ground-breaking book, Colin Shaw opens our eyes to the world of emotions and how to manage them for profit." – **Steve Hurst**, *Managing Editor of* Customer Management

"What is the Customer Experience? While it may be difficult to define, you can be sure that its DNA lies in the way a customer feels – just as this book describes. The real triumph of Colin Shaw's latest title, though, is revealing how unlocking the secrets behind customer emotions can boost your bottom line." – **Claudia Hathaway**, *Editor, CCF and* eCCF

"Positive emotions play a huge but secretive role in retail. The next time your Chief Financial Office says emotions are unimportant, show them this book! Far from being of no value, their influence is immense; ignore them at your peril or use them for profit – the choice is yours." – **Mark Campbell**, *Hamleys Entertainment Manager, Hamleys*

"We are so used to dealing with physical things like price and quality we forget that our customers have emotions. But what should we do about it? Well my congratulations to Colin Shaw for finally enlightening us all with a book that ventures into this new territory and shows us how to make a profit at the same time." – **Alan Gordon**, *Route Director, Stena Line*

"At last here is a business book that tells us the value of emotions and the means of unlocking their potential. For too long now, business leaders have ignored this vital aspect of the customer experience at their peril, but not anymore." – **David West**, *Senior Vice President, Aspect Software*

THE DNA OF CUSTOMER EXPERIENCE

By the same author and published by Palgrave Macmillan:

Revolutionize Your Customer Experience

Building Great Customer Experiences (with John Ivens)

The DNA of Customer Experience
How Emotions Drive Value

Colin Shaw
Founder and CEO of Beyond Philosophy

palgrave
macmillan

First published 2007 by
PALGRAVE MACMILLAN
Houndmills, Basingstoke, Hampshire RG21 6XS and
175 Fifth Avenue, New York, N.Y. 10010
Companies and representatives throughout the world

PALGRAVE MACMILLAN is the global academic imprint of the Palgrave Macmillan division of St. Martin's Press, LLC and of Palgrave Macmillan Ltd. Macmillan® is a registered trademark in the United States, United Kingdom and other countries. Palgrave is a registered trademark in the European Union and other countries.

ISBN-13: 978–0–230–50000–6
ISBN-10: 0–230–50000–5

This book is printed on paper suitable for recycling and made from fully managed and sustained forest sources. Logging, pulping and manufacturing processes are expected to conform to the environmental regulations of the country of origin.

A catalogue record for this book is available from the British Library.

A catalog record for this book is available from the Library of Congress.

10 9 8 7 6 5 4
16 15 14 13 12 11 10 09 08

Printed and bound in Great Britain by
Cromwell Press Limited, Trowbridge, Wiltshire.

Contents

List of Figures and Tables

Figures

Tables

About the Author

Colin Shaw is the founder and CEO of Beyond Philosophy™, the world's thought leaders in the Customer Experience. He is author of two international best selling books, *Building Great Customer Experiences* and *Revolutionize Your Customer Experience*. From their offices in London, England and Atlanta, Georgia in the USA, Colin and his team help organizations improve their Customer Experience. They are proud to have advised the world's top companies including FedEx, Allianz, Barclays, Fireman's Fund, Toyota and T-Mobile as well as Her Majesty's Cabinet Office.

Beyond Philosophy provide the following services:

- **Strategic guidance:** Helping organizations establish strategies using unique methodologies to build a great Customer Experience and generate additional profits.
- **Research:** Thought leading original research to keep you at the forefront of developments in the Customer Experience. In addition, individual research with organizations' customers, with a particular focus on customer emotions.
- **Emotional measurement:** Patented methodologies that measure an organization's emotional engagement with customers.
- **Education:** A range of highly innovative in-house and public educational events to equip organizations with the tools and techniques to enhance your Customer Experience.
- **Conference speaking:** Colin Shaw is a member of the International Federation for Professional Speakers and the Professional Speakers Association and has a reputation for delivering motivational and entertaining speeches that galvanize organizations into wanting to explore the Customer Experience.

There is one fundamental principle for Beyond Philosophy that is encapsulated in the company name. They believe it is OK to have a great thought or idea, but it means nothing unless you go *beyond the philosophy* and do something. Hence the name Beyond Philosophy. Their strengths lie in developing strategy but then, critically, operationalizing that strategy.

Owing to his expertise, Colin has appeared many times as a TV and radio commentator and is quoted in such publications as *The Times*, the *Independent*, *Marketing*, *Marketing Week*, *Customer Management*, *Utility Week* and many other business publications. As a result of his activities, Colin is kindly being called by others "the Guru of the Customer Experience."

Colin has enjoyed over 20 years of experience working in blue-chip companies, including Mars Ltd, Rank Xerox and BT. He has worked at a senior level in a number of different functional areas, including sales, marketing, customer service and training, culminating in his appointment as global SVP, Customer Experience at one of the largest global companies, leading over 3,500 people. This experience gives him a very rounded approach to business – he knows what makes businesses tick and understands the trials and tribulations of running operational units, including the pleasures, the pitfalls, the politics and the policies.

One of Colin's passions is public speaking. His style is very interactive, thought-provoking and amusing. He is an accomplished speaker who has delivered many keynote speeches.

Colin now indulges in his real passions: strategic thinking, developing original concepts, inventing innovative but realistic solutions and critically working out how these can be practically implemented.

Whilst his intellectual rigor is without question, he still manages to keep both feet firmly on the ground. He is most importantly a father of three and husband to Lorraine, his lifelong partner. Colin is a loyal supporter of Luton Town Football (Soccer) Club and collects 1966 World Cup soccer memorabilia.

Beyond Philosophy can be contacted through their offices:

UK Office
212 Piccadilly
London
W1J 9HG
+44 (0)207 917 1717

US Office
Suite 700
One Glenlake Parkway,
Atlanta
Georgia, 30328
(+1)-678-638-6162

www.beyondphilosophy.com

contact@beyondphilosopy.com

Foreword

MAXINE CLARK
Build-A-Bear Workshop

During my third week on the job as an executive trainee, I was fortunate to sit in a room filled with young businesspeople wanting to get ahead in their careers. The May Company CEO at the time was Stanley Goodman. He often talked about retailing as entertainment and the store as a stage. I remember vividly as if he was saying it to me alone "When a customer has fun, they spend more money." This was a defining moment for me and that concept has been with me ever since. Throughout my entire career, my success can be attributed to Stanley sitting on my shoulder reminding me to make it fun!

In 1996 I left corporate America on a mission to bring back the fun to retailing. I was bored by shopping and decided to put my money where my mouth was. I was looking to recreate the excitement and magic I felt as a child when I visited certain stores. Going shopping was an event. You became part of the store, and it was special. The truth is, what it takes to engage and retain retail customers today is really not much different than it was in the past. It's about what I call, good old-fashioned it's-just-about-the-customer retailing.

This holds true for whatever product you sell … it's about the Customer Experience. After all, Ray Kroc didn't invent hamburgers and Howard Schultz didn't invent coffee, they just invented how to sell more and how to sell better. At Build-A-Bear Workshop, we didn't invent teddy bears, we just figured out how to make it more fun!

In any business it's about connecting with your customers and fulfilling a need. But why can't it be fun? This question is explored in Colin Shaw's book, *The DNA of Customer Experience: How Emotions Drive Value*.

At Build-A-Bear Workshop we sell the brand experience – that means we sell not only the product, but the fun and unforgettable memories, which are just as important as the product. Whether it's a family outing, a reward for a job well done in school, or just a fun visit to the mall, we help families spend a special time together.

Each Guest experience is unique, so they come back to the store again and again. Our Guests have so much fun they share their stories with their friends and family members who become future Guests. This viral aspect of our brand is powerful.

We sell our unique products in a dramatic, highly interactive theme-park environment – one with bright colors, larger-than-life fixtures and our own music – an environment that will encourage people to stay and interact with our products and our store associates.

I think we all strive to create successful businesses and brands that connect with our clients, associates and customers. I call it the "cheers" philosophy – you want to go to the place where you feel comfortable, where everyone knows your name ... and you want to come back to it again and again.

At Build-A-Bear Workshop we strive every day to reinvent our company. Whether we're choosing the latest merchandise, selecting new stores or improving our information systems, our focus is to provide our Guests with the best experience we can. And our Guests provide ideas, feedback and great inspiration in the thousands of letters and emails they send us each month. Sometimes they advise us about products ... sometimes they advise us about real estate ... always, their advice is appreciated.

We are a company with heart ... when a Guest makes a stuffed animal in our store, they select a special heart during our signature heart and make a wish ceremony. No two animals are ever alike; no two wishes are ever the same. That's the same way we look at our Guests – each one is unique, each one is special, each one is valued. Our Guests are passionate about and feel ownership in our brand. At Build-A-Bear Workshop our Guests are the heart of our business. They inspire us, they challenge us, they make us smile. Our Guests have come to expect a personal and fun experience every time they shop in our stores, and they won't settle for anything less. We wouldn't have it any other way.

Opportunity to emotionally connect with your customers is everywhere, no matter what your business! I bought a car a few months ago and there was a family in the showroom with kids who were running around the building because they had nothing to keep them occupied. They were so bored. How neat it would have been if the showroom had included an area for kids with play cars and such. In hotels, when families check in, why can't the staff acknowledge the children and make them feel welcome? How hard is it to say "Welcome, how old are you?" Connecting with every Guest is about making people feel respected and connected to your brand. There are a million ways to do it.

As chief executive bear I'm charged with keeping our company a special place. Our Guests are not only our customers, but our vendors, our associates and our shareholders. We believe in always saying yes, and treating each other the way a teddy bear would – it's about being a good person and a good bear. This is the value I see in Colin Shaw's book; he shows us how connecting with each Guest is key to ensuring a great experience. Working with leading academics and statisticians, Colin shows you how to break through barriers and really connect with your customers.

Acknowledgements

Firstly and most importantly, my thanks to the team at Beyond Philosophy for their contributions, however small, in getting this book to market. This includes Joanna Kelly, Karen Malone, Craig Pearce, Sean Freeman, Natalie Kelly, Richard Conklin, Kathryn Brackett, Paula Farney, Jackie Cooper, David Ive, Marc Wall, John Ivens, Eamonn Murray, Simon Povey, Richard Shean, David Solomon and Derek Blackburn.

My specific thanks to the members of the team who have taken the time to review the book and provide me with comments and ideas: Dann Allen, Colin Steventon, Qaalfa Dibeehi and Steven Walden. It is the latter two I would like to single out for a moment. I would particularly like to thank Steven Walden, who leads our research team, for his vital contribution. It has been Steven's role to lead the day-to-day research that underpins this book. It has been a labor of love and extremely well done. Thanks Steven.

Also my thanks to Qaalfa Dibeehi, our vice president of consulting and thought leadership. Qaalfa is blessed with a brain the size of a planet! He has helped us intellectualize what all this means and how we can use this with clients. He has also led the testing with our clients and the development of Emotional Signature™ as a tool that can be used to predict value. Thanks Qaalfa.

My thanks to the extended team: Professor Christopher Voss of the London Business School, for his contribution and guidance; Dr. Jeremy Miles, now of the Rand Corporation, for all the work on the statistics; and Professor Jane Raymond, Bangor University, for her guidance on the psychological aspects of this research.

Thank you to our clients, Darren Cornish, from Norwich Union, for his early thoughts and comments on the development of the Emotional Signature™. My thanks to Memorial Hermann Hospital System for letting us share their Emotional Signature™ and for the unwavering commitment to improve their patients' experience in Houston. Our thanks to David Bradshaw, chief information, planning and marketing officer, Karen Haney, system executive, Customer Experience, and Rhonda Dishongh, director of customer care.

Also similar thanks to IBM for allowing us to share their Emotional Signature™ as well. Thanks to Debra Cross, manager of client experience, Tammy Luke Hughes, client experience consultant, and Tom Dekle, vice president of IBM, your commitment to your clients is very impressive.

My thanks to all our clients who have taken the time and effort to provide commentary for this book: Chuck Kavitsky, formerly CEO of Fireman's Fund Insurance Company, now president of Allianz of America; Simon Fox, formerly MD of Comet and now CEO of HMV; Neville Richardson, CEO, Britannia Building Society; Mark Gater, Customer Experience program manager, Britannia Building Society; also many thanks to Maxine Clark, CEO, Build-A-Bear Workshop, a kindred spirit!

When I look back on my career, there have been a few people who have really influenced me and I would like to take this opportunity to recognize just three. Firstly, a close colleague and old teammate and someone who had a great influence on me, Brady Rafuse. Brady helped me understand marketing in a much deeper way. He has the knack of being able to put across his point in a humorous way, so that I continually learned. I still use his teachings today and I am pleased to say he remains a good friend.

From my past, I would like to thank undoubtedly the best boss I have ever worked for, Neil Hobbs, now a senior executive with Level 3. I remember being interviewed for a marketing role in Neil's team a number of years ago. At that stage I felt my career was in one of those lulls that most careers suffer from. Neil has an amazing gift of spotting the potential in people others do not see. As if this was not enough, he has the additional gift of being able to inspire people to reach their potential. I was one of those people. Neil gave me a break when I needed it, but then, moreover, spent personal time and effort in coaching and developing me. Neil had the foresight to move me from marketing into customer service and thus started my whole interest in the Customer Experience. Without Neil I would not be where I am today, for this I am eternally grateful to him. However, probably the best news is that now Neil is a good friend, the kind you know you can rely on if you have a problem, and that means more to me than anything else. There are not many people like that in the world.

From the present I would like to sincerely thank my partner David Ive. I remember the first day I told Dave of my plans to leave my highly paid job and set up Beyond Philosophy. He has been 110% supportive, and joined Beyond Philosophy full time a year or so later. I always joke that Dave does the "boring stuff," finance, supplier management, legal work, and so on. The real joke is that we all know these are really not boring, but vital. Dave performs this role exceptionally well. I consider Dave to be my "wise owl"; having run many successful small businesses there is nothing that surprises him. His counsel is first-class and the biggest accolade I can give him is that I trust him implicitly. Furthermore, I know that Dave would not be able to function and support me so avidly without the constant support and understanding of his family, so thank you to his wife Sue and children Andrew, Sarah, Michelle, and Nicola. But more important than all this, Lorraine and I are pleased to say that Dave and Sue are good family friends and I know if anything happened to Lorraine and me, they would take care of our kids, as we would theirs. Thanks Dave and Sue!

On a personal level I would like to thank as always my friends and extended family, named in previous books, especially my Dad, for their support and continued understanding of my absence while writing. Thanks also to Derek,

Mandy, Amy and Dan Morgan for the use of their Florida home so I could write in the sunshine! Most of all, though, I would like to thank my wife Lorraine and my kids Coralie, Ben and Abbie. Building Beyond Philosophy from scratch five years ago into an organization that now turns over seven figures, with offices in the UK and the US, has not been an easy task and takes some effort. When you throw on top of that writing three books and traveling across the pond 15 times a year, you can imagine the effect on my family. Lorraine and my kids have been very supportive and encouraged me along the way, as they know this is important to me. Without their understanding and support none of this would be possible. Thank you and I love you all dearly.

COLIN SHAW

Introduction

PROFESSOR CHRIS VOSS
London Business School

I have been leading a team of researchers at the London Business School via the Advanced Institute of Management research (AIM) to study the emergent field of the "Experience Economy" because the development of the Customer Experience is a key innovation in business. In today's environment of ever-more sophisticated consumers, those who deliver memorable Customer Experiences consistently create superior value and competitive advantage. This is true in the business-to-business situation as well. Indeed the creation of these experiences is increasingly becoming both the leading edge and a standard practice for business. Some examples include:

- Lego giving children the opportunity to play with their toys in shops and, importantly, providing parents with the opportunity to experience their children playing with Lego toys.
- Zara creating a sense of anticipation in their clothing shops driving customers to repeat visit 17 times per year versus the 3–4 for regular stores.
- Joi de Vivre theming its boutique hotels from movies to Rolling Stones.
- Knoll Group developing a museum, not only dealerships and showrooms, for its business buyers.

These businesses and many others like them are examples of companies that have begun to address the five imperatives for managing experiences:

1. Manage experience as theatre
2. Use experience to build brand equity
3. Balance control and spontaneity
4. Manage conflict between creativity and business
5. Develop and use appropriate measures.

However, the financial assessment of experience is often buried under multiple layers in an organization and can be difficult to identify, with organizations often claiming that experiences offer intangible rather than tangible benefits. The exciting thing about the Emotional Signature™ is that it is the first robust measurement system that assesses the emotional part of customer experiences! I choose my words carefully. This is the first system designed for use in the business world systematically tested and shown to be accurate. Thus, the Emotional Signature™ can help businesses develop and use appropriate measures, one of the five imperatives for managing experiences. Furthermore, it provides an estimate of the financial implications of having a particular emotional signature.

A good example of this is in the way businesses manage "delight" and "outrage." In the former, the need to "delight" customers has become part of the rhetoric of service marketing and a common key objective of customer experience strategy. Delight is typically seen as exceeding customer expectations, and surprise. Maurice Sardi, CEO of the Knoll Group (a leading US manufacturer of office furniture), for example, has defined "delight" as "meeting customer needs and then going beyond them – building in qualities like personality, fun, and surprise."

Research has shown that delight is associated with positive emotions and cannot be achieved without surprisingly positive levels of performance. Delight can occur either on a one-time basis or through continued raising of customer expectations, which makes it more difficult to delight the customer in the future. Similar findings are reported on outrage, at the other end of the scale. Focusing on delight and outrage, which are associated with more intense emotions than are satisfaction and dissatisfaction, may lead to a deeper understanding of the dynamics of customer emotions and their effect on behavior and loyalty.

In general, therefore, rational delight is a necessary but not sufficient condition for customers to display extreme positive behavior such as actively recommending a business. Rational delight is related to customer satisfaction. Thus, satisfaction typically tells us about the rational experience, not about the full experience (that is, rational and emotional). To resolve this issue, Beyond Philosophy's Emotional Signature™ allows us, for the first time, to gauge the emotional experience of customers. This is necessary for businesses to understand what delights their customers.

I worked with Beyond Philosophy on the Emotional Signature™ research. I met with the guys from Beyond Philosophy several times, along with their statistician, Dr. Jeremy Miles. The methodology used is sound and the statistics rigorous and I am happy to endorse this work. As the results were analyzed, the implications were jumping off the page. This work really has identified emotional precursor factors of delight and outrage – the drivers and destroyers of experience-based value.

The implications are that a business can now assess the full Customer Experience. Satisfaction still holds sway in measuring the rational experience while Emotional Signature™ gauges the emotional experience. As we move forward we will better understand how these two are related and drive sensitive outcome measures like the Fred Reichheld/Satmetrix Net Promoter® Score.

The successful company examples I started off with (Lego, Zara, and so on) benefit from being among the first companies to specify their Customer Experience. As more and more companies address their Customer Experience issues, it will be more and more difficult for those businesses to develop experiences which differentiate them. As this happens, accurate information on the complete Customer Experience will become ever-more important. It will be exciting to witness the evolution of the Emotional Signature™ as businesses take it on and begin to work on the emotional experience.

1 Moving from a Religion to a Financial Imperative

You may not be responsible for the past but you are responsible for the future. (Anon)

The names of the airline, airports and destinations of this experience have been changed to ensure the anonymity of the people involved. This was an actual experience of mine.

"Would all those passengers on the AAE Airline flight to Marbella in Spain please report outside immediately as the coach will be leaving shortly to take you to London's Stansted Airport."

"What?" I said to my wife Lorraine, "Did you hear that? What is happening?" Somewhat annoyed and frustrated I rushed over to the counter and asked what was happening. All we knew was that when we arrived at the airport at 7.30 that morning we were told the flight had been delayed "due to technical problems."

On reaching the desk I interrupted an AAE employee who was chatting to her friend. "Excuse me, what is happening with our flight?" "Didn't you hear the announcement?" she said in a tone of voice that was really saying, are you stupid and why are you disturbing me? "The flight has been cancelled and we are putting on another plane so you'll be flying out from Stansted," she said nonchalantly as if it was an everyday occurrence. "You had better get out there quickly before the coach leaves."

I hurried back to where Lorraine and I had set up camp. We quickly gathered our belongings, leaving our coffee and Danish pastries as we were now feeling somewhat stressed and concerned that we were going to miss the coach.

However, we should have known it was a case of "hurry up and wait."

Acting like sheep we followed the crowd. I noted there was no one to guide us. We joined the chaos that was meant to be a line. There was one coach and everyone was trying to get on it. I noticed two AAE employees happily chatting together, totally oblivious to the chaos around them. I thought to myself how funny it is that you find yourself resenting them being happy when you, the customer, are feeling all these negative emotions. It amazed me that customers were loading their own bags onto the coach with no help from the driver or the AAE employees; they just continued to laugh and chat.

Some of the people who had loaded their bags got on the coach only to discover there were no seats left. As no one was in control it was chaos! These passengers then had to unload their bags, by themselves, causing more delays.

I thought of my coffee and Danish pastry and cursed myself for allowing myself to get panicked into coming outside and waiting in the cold. After 45 minutes of waiting, another coach arrived, after which a similar farce ensued. We finally loaded our bags and got on the coach. There was no apology from the AAE employees, no reason given for

1

the delay and no announcement about what was happening or when the flight was leaving, so no one could plan pickups. It was clear they just didn't care and only wanted to see the back of us as soon as they could.

It's interesting how this kind of episode brought down the barriers and people started "bonding" with each other. All our fellow passengers recounted their stories of what had happened to them, what they had been told and the impact it would have on them.

We arrived at Stansted where there was no one to greet us. We walked to departures and we were asked to join a line by an AAE employee who was directing people at the check-in area. After 30 minutes' wait, we finally reached the head of the line! Thank goodness. We were there now.

"Tickets please," the woman said in that sort of way that you know she just wanted to go home. Her job was to process us. "You're not booked in on this flight," she proudly announced in a loud voice. "What!" we replied totally exasperated. "Look, we have just transferred over from Luton and we have been up since 6.00 this morning." I could sense the frustration and annoyance building in me. I am normally very mild mannered and it takes a lot to get me angry, but I could feel the anger rising in me. She then looked at the screen and said "Ah, you're in the wrong line," again in a tone of voice that said Ah, I am right and you were wrong … Told you so!

"This line is the flight to Marbella from Stansted," she said in triumph. "You'll have to go over there to that line." Confused, I protested that we were in Stansted and we were going to Marbella. With a wry smile she said "Ah yes but you have transferred from Luton, this is the Stansted to Marbella flight, and you need the Luton to Marbella flight." By this stage, I could feel the anger welling up inside me. "But we were told to come here by that AAE woman," I said, pointing an accusing finger. "Well, you need to line up over there."

I thought maybe another tack would be better, so I put on my "lost boy" look and said "But can't you just book us in from this line?" "NO." came the sharp reply. "Listen, you're lucky we have even put a flight on for you today, and we (Stansted) didn't have to." That was the straw that broke the camel's back; she had the audacity to tell me that they were doing us a favor! At this point I decided to give her some free consultancy and angrily told her what I thought about the service she was providing. I told her that we, the inconvenient customers, paid her wages. There was a spontaneous round of applause from other passengers around us.

It was obvious that we weren't going to win, so we moved lines. By then I was really mad. Not just the incompetence, but the total lack of care had enraged me.

We were confronted by another long line and a further 30-minute wait. We decided to complain to the manager. On three separate occasions we were informed that we had to go to the check-in desk to meet the manager as she "couldn't come out onto the floor." We refused and eventually the manager agreed to talk to us in the line. To be fair she listened and, for the first time that day, we had an apology. She informed us that they were an outsourced company and couldn't do anything and that if we wanted to complain we should email our complaint to their customer services.

We were the last to get on the plane and for all this trouble we received a £6 ($10) meal voucher with which we had to buy sandwiches as there was no time to eat before we got on the plane.

Lorraine and I were now feeling a mixture of emotions. Relief was the main one, but also resentment and frustration at how we had been treated. The delay was bad enough, but these things happen; it was the manner in which we were treated that really annoyed us.

Here's the irony though. We were catching this flight to go to our mountain retreat to write this book! It was as if someone had said, "OK let's give you a case study to talk about."

After a good week of writing and an uneventful trip home, I decided to complain and instead of writing found it easier to phone the call center to complain. After what seemed an eternity the call was answered and I was informed nothing could be done without the booking reference number. I protested that surely they could look up the flight and my name. No. Incidentally, whilst I was complaining, AAE was making money on the national rate number (an 0870 number in the UK – which means the company shares the profit with the telecoms supplier), which they had decided to use on their "customer service" line. This is always a telltale sign for me, when a company effectively makes a profit from their customer complaints! They suggested I write an email with all the details. Over a three-month period I wrote three times to the customer service team and didn't even get an acknowledgement! Finally I sent a letter to the CEO by recorded delivery. No reply. A month later I sent another one. Finally, on 14 October, five months after my original emails of complaint, I received a reply from a customer service representative. I'm not sure if this was replying to my previous emails or my letters to the CEO. It was a standard reply and didn't address the complaint in my correspondence. So I gave up.

Let me be very clear about the issues with this experience. It is not the fact the aircraft had technical problems, this can happen. Nor is it the fact we were transferred to another airport. It is the total lack of care and consideration demonstrated by all the employees of this airline, during and after this experience. They couldn't care less, and I was an inconvenience to them. This is why I have told many people of this experience and advised them not to fly with AAE.

Why do organizations provide experiences like this? Why do they treat customers with such disdain? Why do they focus on themselves and not the customer? Clearly, it must be because they consider this is the best way to make a buck. In our experience, typically, these organizations are run by management that are inwardly focused and blinded by their short-term focus on profits, so much so it's not even worth raising the subject of Customer Experience with them. As markets commoditize, organizations struggle to differentiate themselves, and unless you are in a growing market, as in the case of budget airlines in Europe, this can adversely affect your bottom line and, as a consequence, shareholder value.

How are organizations responding to this challenge? Well, if you only have a hammer you think everything is a nail. In the same way, the old guards of senior execs' only response to these conditions is to do the same things but faster and more aggressively. The irony is that this drives commoditization further and quicker. The knock-on effect is a personal one for the old guard as eventually they are replaced with someone who can deal with these issues. We have all seen the tenure of CEOs reducing each year as they struggle to produce the returns required. It is no surprise therefore that you hear the desperate cry from the old guard throughout the organization:

Show me the money!

At the same time we are seeing a new breed of enlightened, customer-focused executives who knowingly smile, and see the answer as simple. Focus on the customer, not the organization, and by doing so this will give you a differentiator, increased profits and a higher shareholder value. They understand, as we outlined in our previous books *Building Great Customer Experiences* and *Revolutionize Your Customer Experience*,[1] that the Customer Experience is the next competitive battleground and over 50% of an experience is emotions. Thus, provide customers with an emotionally engaging experience and the rest will take care of itself. We hope that as you are one of this growing band of enlightened leaders, and with the guidance of this and our previous books, you will understand how to enjoy the benefits this will undoubtedly bring.

We have been fortunate to work with some great people and organizations from around the globe that we will refer to throughout this book. You will read of five case studies of established organizations, dealing in mature markets, who are now building emotionally engaging experiences. You will read of their increase in revenues and profits. For example, one of these organizations, TNT (a large courier), which has enjoyed 100% growth in revenues, doubled its customer base, substantially reduced customer churn, increased the effectiveness of its marketing campaigns by 20% and reduced employee attrition by 13%. All this was achieved by understanding the DNA, the detail, of the Customer Experience and how emotions drive value. If you want to find out how, read on; if you want to find out what you need to do to provide an emotionally engaging experience, read on; if you want to find out how you can financially justify a Customer Experience program, read on. You'll be pleased to know you have chosen the right book!

In our quest to continue to provide thought leadership in the area of Customer Experience, following 18 months of ground-breaking research in the UK and USA, we are pleased to reveal that we have discovered four clusters of emotions that drive and destroy value for an organization. We have discovered that every organization has a previously undetected *Emotional Signature*™ embedded in their Customer Experience that affects value generation.[2] This signature is unique to every organization and can be one of the underlying reasons for good or bad revenue performance. For the first time anywhere in the world, that we are aware of, we can now demonstrate an empirical link between evoking certain emotions and increasing or decreasing revenue.

We have discovered that one of these clusters of emotions drives short-term spend in customers and the other three drive or destroy customer loyalty. They will also increase or decrease your Net Promoter® Score (NPS); which we discuss in greater detail in Chapter 8.[3] This, then, can be used to reduce customer churn. We will reveal a simple way of measuring customer emotions and understanding what your Emotional Signature™ is. The big breakthrough is that you will then be able to show the accountants how much this signature is worth financially to your organization. For the first time we will be able to "show them the money!" and even convince the old guard they need to change.

Let us start by looking at my experience with the budget airline outlined at the beginning of this chapter. We are sure you could recount similar experiences to the one described above, times when you have felt angry and frustrated during a Customer Experience. Do you feel loyal to these types of organizations? How many people have you told of your poor experience? You may be aware that on average people tell about nine other people of a poor experience. On the other hand, we know that retaining the same customer is much more profitable than finding a new one. It therefore makes economic sense to provide a good Customer Experience. If this is the case, why do organizations get themselves into this mess?

If I was to replay my experience to the senior team at AAE Airline, do you think the execs would say "Great, that's exactly what is meant to happen!" I think not. This example just highlights how organizations really get things wrong. The budget airlines in Europe are still enjoying a growing market with new destinations and lots of new passengers discovering they can fly abroad for a cheap weekend or vacation.

Due to this growth, at the moment, they can get away with providing a poor experience and people will still fly with them. However, as they reach market saturation, they will soon realize that it is not just about gaining new customers but retaining existing ones. This is exactly what happened to the mobile phone (cellular) market in Europe a few years ago. In the late 1990s and early 2000s it enjoyed massive growth and effectively couldn't care less about the Customer Experience. Now customer churn is killing profitability and manufacturers are all trying to improve their Customer Experience.

As we outlined in our previous books, the big issue that faces business today is that everything is the same. Organizations are selling similar products and services to the same people. This, along with massive improvements in technology and more efficient offshore manufacturing, enables price reduction, which drives commoditization which in turn drives down profits and ultimately shareholder value. This is why 95% of senior business leaders believe the Customer Experience is the next competitive battleground.[4] One of our clients, Simon Fox, MD of Comet, a large electrical retailer in the UK, faced this challenge and shares the views of the more enlightened senior executives:

Comet operates in a hugely price competitive environment with new sources of competition emerging all the time. On one hand the internet, on the other supermarkets. Comet's role is as a specialist; a deep range specialist and as such it was under threat from both directions. It seemed to us that what Comet really needed to do was to re-establish its position as a specialist. We have large stores with extensive ranges and competitive prices but what we were not focusing on was providing customers with a really great shopping experience and helping them cut through the confusion and complexities of electricals.

I saw this as the most important part of our strategy. The Customer Experience is at the heart of that strategy as it is the one way we could differentiate ourselves from our competitors, therefore the whole business had to orientate around it. For instance, our advertising changed as a direct result of our work, putting the customer and the Customer Experience at the heart of the business. We relaunched the brand; new colors and new logo in August 2005.

Many of our other clients will tell you a similar story. We have been fortunate to deal with many of the world's leading organizations, such as IBM, Allianz, RBS (Royal Bank of Scotland), Virgin Mobile, Microsoft, and Royal Bank of Canada. In so doing we have discovered that you need to dig into the detail and understand the DNA of Customer Experience.

In this book we will look at this DNA. We will look at what the Emotional Signature™ is for business as a whole, different sectors and individual organizations. We will delve down into the detail of their DNA and dissect what is happening. We also go an important stage further. We reveal what you need to do to improve.

With our expert eye, gained from many successful implementations, a great deal of research and the countless analyses of different organizations' experiences, we can reveal what they are doing to cause a poor experience or to provide a great experience. We will be able to enlighten you in what you need to do to change. For example, clearly AAE is an example of a poor experience. We would also judge from this experience that there is a lack of care of the customer which is endemic throughout the organization and potentially the budget airline sector. The CEO at AAE hasn't even had the decency to reply to or acknowledge my letters – it is obvious he doesn't care. Another CEO of a budget airline, when interviewed in the media about its poor levels of customer service, proudly said "What do you expect if you pay £30 ($54)?" In both these examples, consider what this says about the DNA of these organizations? What DNA does it reveal? It clearly reveals a "couldn't care less" attitude to customers for both carriers.

As a result, what attitude do you think the employees in both organizations have towards customers? The answer; a poor one. This attitude is written into the DNA of these organizations and manifests itself in their Emotional Signature™ and their Customer Experience. It is embedded deep and is hereditary. It's like knowing that every male in your family is going to go bald or unfortunately have some hereditary illness. This DNA in organizations is passed from generation to generation and becomes an inherited trait. Long-serving employees pass this DNA down to new employees. For example:

I was once running a "Philosophers Day" in a utility company; the objective was for them to understand what the Customer Experience is about, why it is important and to devise a plan of what they need to do to improve. The delegates were a group of seasoned senior managers who had been with the company for a few years. Also present was a new, enthusiastic woman who had just joined from another company. We were discussing the poor experience this organization was providing and debating the causes. Everyone was agreeing on the issues which had been around for some time. The new woman was enthusiastically suggesting solutions to the problem but each of these was rejected by the group, typically saying "we tried that before and it didn't work." Eventually the DNA was passed to the woman as she decided it was too much effort to swim against the tide and decided not to suggest any further solutions. The culture of the organization was effectively trained into her that day and she decided to accept this rather than fight.

We are sure AAE is no different and the DNA has been handed down from person to person. In our last book *Revolutionize Your Customer Experience*, we reveal a model called Naïve to Natural™ which showed how oriented around the customer an organization is. There are four stages of this model, Naïve, Transactional, Enlightened and Natural. We would categorize AAE as being Naïve[5] and the company typically will have a poor Emotional Signature™. The issue for AAE is that its attitude becomes embedded in its genes, it's part of who it is, its trait, its makeup, its DNA. No surprise then that it provides a poor experience. Therefore, there is an opportunity for other airlines to differentiate themselves on their Customer Experience. We are potentially seeing the very early signs of this happening with one airline proudly presenting their tag line in a recent ad:

Cutting fares, not service

Our research shows that the Naïve organizations of this world, like AAE, will ultimately be forced to undertake major genetic reengineering as their market becomes more and more competitive and they struggle for differentiation. When this happens they will find this reengineering is a long, complex and costly procedure. For example, they will need to remove people who are of the wrong genetic makeup and review their recruitment policies. They will need to redesign their process with the customer and not the organization in mind. They will need to implement a major training program on how to be customer focused. This type of change is painful, resource hungry and costly. All this, because they did not start with the customer in mind at the beginning.

On the opposite end of the model are Natural[5] organizations that have a DNA gene structure that means they naturally have a positive Emotional Signature™. These are organizations like Mandarin Oriental Hotels, Harley-Davidson, Krispy Kremes, Pret a Manger, Disney, and so on. Their DNA makes them provide a naturally great experience.

If we are to change your organization, then the first thing you need to do is understand the DNA of the Customer Experience. Then, and only then, can you start to undertake genetic engineering to solve the problem forever.

Ask yourself what is the DNA of your Customer Experience? What is your Emotional Signature™? How is it made up? How is it created? Let us look a bit more into the detail. When human life is created, our DNA contains 23 chromosomes from the male and 23 from the female which combine to create a unique individual. In the case of an experience, it is not male and female, it is customer and organization that come together to create an experience.

From the organizational view point, there are a mixture of many things: their mission, vision, the characteristics and beliefs of the leadership team, how this team role model behavior, what market they operate in, what the employees are like and so on and so forth.

To understand the DNA of the Customer Experience, we need first to understand what a Customer Experience is. Here is our definition, which you may well recognize from our previous books:

> A Customer Experience is an interaction between an organization and a customer. It is a blend of an organization's physical performance, the senses stimulated and emotions evoked, each intuitively measured against customer expectations across all moments of contact.

A Customer Experience is about a number of things. It about a physical Customer Experience, such as price, product, location, opening times, and the channel that is used, that is, stores, online, telephone, the features of the product, and so on. Critically it is also about emotions – how a customer feels. Our research shows that over 50% of a Customer Experience is about emotions. Maxine Clark is CEO of the highly successful Build-A-Bear Workshop. Emotions are embedded into the design of their great experience. Let us hear what Maxine has to say:

> Emotions are a key part of our offering and something we have deliberately designed into our experience. We want to connect with our Guests and make sure that they build a connection with their bear so they make a new friend for life. Connecting on an emotional level is an important part of the brand experience.

Maxine is trying to positively affect their Emotional Signature™ by connecting at an emotional level with their guests. One way that they do that, and a sign for us of a sophisticated experience designer like Maxine and the team at Build-A-Bear Workshop, is when they design into their experience the use of senses: sight, sound, taste, smell and touch. They know this is the only way that humans can acquire information. Without senses we do not gain any information. Customers are then very inventive with this; Maxine gives us a great example:

> We make a difference in the lives of our Guests and they connect to us in ways we couldn't even imagine. Guests use our Build-A-Sound, where you can record your own sound, in many imaginative ways. A new mother will take it to the doctor's office for the ultrasound and record her new baby's heartbeat, then she makes a bear with that heartbeat that she'll have forever. Other Guests have recorded the sound of the baby after it's born so the grandparents can have a bear with the child's first cry in it. We wouldn't have thought that up.

The sophisticated designer also knows that the Customer Experience is across all moments of contact, so it's not just one part of the organization; the "customer journey" can touch many parts of an organization. We may see an advertisement and then visit a website, followed by going into a store, then have something delivered, deal with or contact customer services and so on – a number of different contact points.

In our experience organizations are obsessed with the physical aspects of their Customer Experience. They have meeting after meeting about the delivery timescales, lead times, range of products, the time it takes to answer a phone call, the cost of the mailer going to customers, bill inserts, and so on. But ask yourself this: if 50% of a Customer Experience is about emotions, how many meetings do you have where you discuss the emotions that you are evoking in your customers? How many meetings do you have where you truly debate the emotional impact your experience is having? How many meetings do you have when you are discussing or reviewing the DNA of your Customer Experience?

The financial services market is highly competitive with very few organizations providing an outstanding Customer Experience. Most organizations we work with are looking to solve problems; only a few are looking at this as an opportunity to differentiate. One of our clients, Neville Richardson, the CEO of Britannia Building Society, a large financial services company in the UK (similar to a saving and loan company in the US), explains his view:

> We started the work on the Customer Experience, not because we thought we had a problem, but because we thought there was an opportunity. Having spent a great deal of time on replacing all our core systems, undertaking a great deal of work on our culture, values and strategy, we felt all these things combined to give us the capability to provide a very different experience based on an emotional level.

It is unusual for a CEO and a board to be talking about an "emotional experience" but this is what needs to happen. It doesn't occur overnight. Typically we find there is a period of adjustment that needs to take place before emotions become accepted in an organization's vocabulary. Mark Gater, Customer Experience program manager, Britannia Building Society, sums it up:

> If you asked me 24 months ago if I'd be standing up in front of senior managers openly talking about deliberately evoking feelings in customers, I would have told you that you were mad! It probably took me about three months to even get comfortable talking about this and that's from somebody absolutely immersed in it. It's not an easy journey for people to take because it's not something you talk about in business, is it? In business you talk about profits and money!

It is strange, as emotions are with us every day of the week in our private lives, but not in business. Let's try a test. As 50% of an experience is about emotions, what are the emotions you are trying to evoke? Write them down now. Now on the next occasion you meet a colleague, or your boss, ask them to do the same. As Mark says, I bet the first thing they will do is look at you as if you are mad! The second thing, when they realize you are serious, is that they will all come up with different emotions. If 50% of a Customer Experience is about emotions, then why are you leaving this to chance? It's like leaving your pricing strategy to chance.

Emotions drive human behavior!

Emotions are at the very core of all the actions we take and yet for years businesses have ignored them. We always refer to this looking at the core emotions as an "onion." An onion has many layers and you have to "peel back the onion" to go through the different layers to get to the core. For example, consider the cars that people drive. It is not as simple as "I want a car that carries me from A to B." People buy cars that are impractical just so they can enjoy the ride, or that say something about their social status. Other people can become envious or jealous, which drives them to gossip negatively about the person. Think about the clothes you wear. Again they say something about you – what group you belong to, if you like to be seen as smart or casual or in what context, all driven by emotions of self-worth. Emotions drive our daily lives. People take holidays to feel relaxed or maybe an adventure holiday to be challenged or feel exhilarated. We also buy from organizations that we trust, even if it's only buying a Mars bar. Emotions are at the core of our being.

But here is the dilemma. In our experience most people will agree that a significant part of the Customer Experience is about emotions. Some argue the percentage of impact but logic tells you that emotions form part of it. The issue becomes, what effects do they have and how do you "manage" these? It is a lot easier to design a logical, physical process. Planning to evoke emotions in customers is far more difficult. This takes us back to the old guard and the enlightened execs. In our experience the old guard need a lot of convincing that this is the right way to go and will produce the right results. Let me give you an example:

We were engaged by one of the world's largest insurance companies to carry out a Naïve to Natural® assessment on 16 of their companies around the world. They wanted to see how well these companies were orientated towards the customer and identify best practice. They had realized they needed to improve their Customer Experience to reduce churn and to differentiate themselves in the market.

We were constantly being challenged, and rightly so, on the likely impact of a Customer Experience initiative on revenues. The board member we dealt with, and the central project team, all intuitively understood that improving the Customer Experience was the right thing to do and emotions absolutely formed part of this. Others in the organization were less convinced. A typical situation we encounter daily. We were particularly being challenged on our thoughts on emotions. The skeptics wanted to see a demonstrable link between improving their experience and increase in revenues. I particularly remember the day we were presenting the findings of our Naïve to Natural® assessment and an action plan to improve their experience to the board of one of their companies in Europe. We had been warned that we were in for a rough time as they were not convinced that the Customer Experience would help them improve their revenues.

Everyone listened very intently to our presentation. One of the board members then said something that was to stay with me for some time. He said "Thank you for your presentation, but I am still not convinced that this will help us improve our profitability. The trouble is that you (Beyond Philosophy and the client's central team) look at this as a religion. Like any religion you either believe it or you don't. For those who do believe it, there is no question that this is the right approach and you probably can't understand why people are even questioning this. For those who don't believe it, and I am one of them, I need more proof that this will work as I do not have your faith. I cannot see a demonstrable link between evoking customer emotions and improving our revenues and without this I cannot support this."

He was right. To those of us who had "seen the light" it was obvious. To him it wasn't. That is not his fault; it is ours because we had not explained it well enough in terms that he could understand. We constantly find that if you believe then nothing else matters, you don't need evidence, you take things on faith, like any religion. This discussion really made me think. We need to find a way to empirically link how evoking emotions in customers gives a financial return. Answering this one question has taken us over two years of hard work. But we now have the answer and it is already proving to be valuable for many of our clients.

We are frequently contacted by people who have read our books and are looking for guidance on how to improve their experience. Typically they are fellow converts who understand the many benefits that improving the experience will have for an organization. The chances are that you are one of them as you are taking the time and trouble to read this book. The issue you will face is convincing others of your beliefs, especially the leadership. Chuck Kavitsky, CEO Fireman's Fund Insurance Company in the USA, and another client, gives us his view:

That doesn't happen unless you have leadership that is engaged, that is absolutely unwavering in its confidence in the Customer Experience. If leadership is not engaged then it won't work.

This book has been inspired by the challenges we have received to prove that emotions drive value. We have focused on changing this from a religion into a financial imperative that is so compelling you would need to be mad not to believe it. It is about looking at things from a financial perspective and providing a demonstrable link that we struggled with two years ago. It's about pushing the boundaries of our understanding on the subject of Customer Experience and continuing to provide thought leadership in this area, understanding the DNA of Customer Experience, and how emotions drive value.

11

Over this period we have had many debates with leading gurus around the world. We have debated this with many CEOs, some of whose contributions you will read in this book. All these organizations are improving the Customer Experience and achieving greater financial returns, all have a story to tell but all of them are doing it ultimately for one reason; to make money. Let's hear again from Neville Richardson, Britannia Building Society. Neville is one of those rare CEOs who knows that improving the Customer Experience is the right strategic move:

> You asked if we produced a business case for this work. Being an accountant by background I could have prepared some high-level assumptions and produced a compelling business plan that would have convinced anyone that the Customer Experience was the right thing to do. A number of people on the board were pushing for this but I resisted very hard as I felt this was just strategically the right thing to do. We didn't need a massive business case to prove it. What I do know is that if we reduced our complaint levels by say ten percent of our first time resolution, then these numbers would be big enough to justify it financially. But that's not the point, this is the right thing to do for our customers.

It is not for the Nevilles of this world that we undertook this work. Unfortunately Neville is in the minority of CEOs and we certainly wish there were more people like him to champion this work from his level. This is for the others who may need a bit more convincing. To do this let's go back to first principles for a moment, let's stop and consider what organizations want to do:

- Produce loyal customers
  - Loyal customers are cheaper to serve than new customers
- Attract new customers at least cost
  - Word of mouth and referrals are the cheapest and most effective form of advertising
- Reduce costs as far as possible
  - Cut out waste and inefficiency
- Increase spend by getting people to buy more
  - Loyal customers spend more money with the companies they are loyal to.

How can the Customer Experience help to achieve these aims? Well the good news is, in many ways, but only when you understand the DNA of the Customer Experience and you look into the detail of what is happening.

To understand the DNA of the Customer Experience, we have been studying in minute detail the connection between customer emotions and the effect on loyalty and spend. We have interviewed over a thousand people on both sides of the Atlantic. We are pleased that this has been very much a team effort. We have been fortunate enough to be guided by Professor Jane Raymond, one of the UK's leading psychologists and chair of experimental

12

consumer psychology, and Dr. Jeremy Miles, now of the Rand Corporation and author of two books on statistics, who have helped us discover the links between the drivers and the destroyers of value. And finally we thank the London Business School for the guidance, advice, and support of Professor Christopher Voss. He has challenged us, input his own ideas and thoughts, and endorsed our methodology and discovery. Not to make this just an academic exercise, we have also tested this with a number of clients in live situations, some of whom you will read about in this book. Truly a team effort.

As you will see in Figure 1.1, there are three clusters that drive value and one cluster that destroys value. While these clusters are statistically independent, our experience shows that there is a natural order of these clusters. We have dedicated a chapter to each of these but let us give you a little taster now.

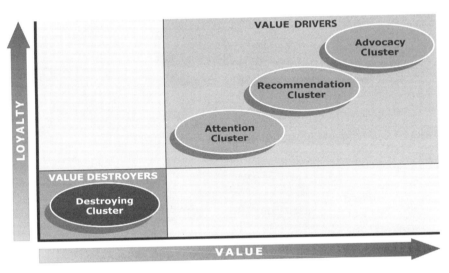

Figure 1.1 Emotional Signature of value

The Destroying Cluster of emotions is the first place you need to focus on when looking to improve your Customer Experience. There will be a number of actions your organization undertakes that, knowingly or unknowingly, are evoking these emotions. We are not naive enough to believe you will be able to eradicate the destroying emotions entirely, but they do need controlling. This cluster not only destroys value but it also costs you money, for example dealing with customer complaints, returns, and so on.

There are three clusters that drive value.

The Attention Cluster contains the emotions that have a proven link to increased customer spend. Our research shows that if you evoke the emotions in this cluster, your customers will spend more money with you in the short term. This cluster can give you a temporary high and attract customers to your organization.

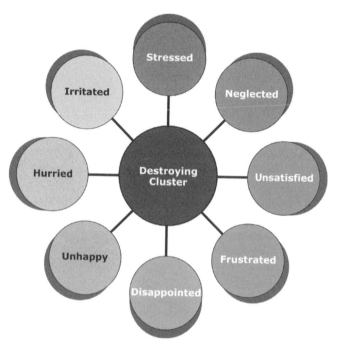

Figure 1.2 Destroying Cluster of emotions

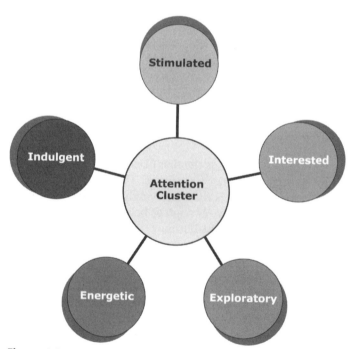

Figure 1.3 Attention Cluster of emotions

If you want to start to have loyal customers and build a long-term relationship with customers, then you need to focus on the Recommendation and Advocacy Clusters of emotions. Taking the Recommendation Cluster (Figure 1.4) first, we have called it this to reflect the fact that it is about gaining customers who will recommend you. This also links to the Net Promoter® Score. Therefore, evoking these emotions will create loyal customers and will improve your NPS. We also named this cluster "Recommendation" to reflect the fact that this is more of a *reactive* state. For instance, if a friend or colleague asks who you could recommend, then you can tell them, but you may not proactively tell them.

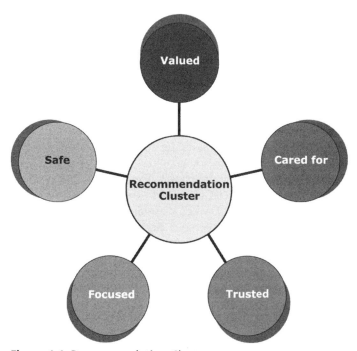

Figure 1.4 Recommendation Cluster

The Advocacy Cluster only contains two emotions as you will see in Figure 1.5. If a customer is an advocate, they *proactively* tell people about your organization without prompting. Surely this is our aim, as it's the cheapest form of marketing there is. These, then, are the ultimate drivers of customer loyalty and your NPS.

We hope this gives you a brief overview of these clusters. As we get further into the book, we will give you a more detailed view and describe what you can do to evoke these emotions in your customers. Let's hear what Maxine Clark, CEO Build-A-Bear Workshop, says on how they are using these emotions to good effect:

We sell our unique products in a dramatic, highly interactive theme-park environment –

Figure 1.5 Advocacy Cluster

one with bright colors, larger-than-life fixtures and our own music – an environment that encourages people to stay and interact with our products and our store associates. I think we all strive to create successful businesses and brands that connect with our clients, associates and customers. I call it the "cheers" philosophy – you want to go to the place where you feel comfortable, where everyone knows your name … and you want to come back to it again and again.

As you are talking about in this book – the emotions that drive spend and loyalty, things like customers feeling interested, stimulated, energetic, being cared for, and being valued – these things all apply and are used at Build-A-Bear Workshop.

As you see from Maxine's comments, they have thought through the design of their Customer Experience. It is important that these emotions are embedded into that design to enjoy some of the returns you will read about in this book. To do that we believe it is beneficial for you to further understand the DNA of your Customer Experience by understanding how a person is made up. By so doing we hope you will gain an understanding of what we are recommending and why we are making the recommendations we are. Therefore, let us take a look at the whole subject of emotions, where they come from, what effect they have on your customers, and what this means for you and your organization.

Notes

1. *Building Great Customer Experiences*, C. Shaw and J. Ivens (2004) Basingstoke, Palgrave Macmillan and *Revolutionize Your Customer Experience*, C. Shaw (2005) Basingstoke, Palgrave Macmillan.
2. Emotional Signature™ is a trademarked methodology for which the patent is pending.
3. Net Promoter® is a registered trademark of Fred Reichheld, Satmetrix and Bain and company.
4. Market Forum Research 2002 – The Next Competitive Battleground.
5. The Naïve to Natural model, a comprehensive review of the orientation of the organization toward the customer in *Revolutionize Your Customer Experience*.

2 The DNA of a Customer

Chuck Kavitsky, CEO, Fireman's Fund Insurance Company, in the US:

My youngest daughter was driving in San Francisco when a person ran a red light and hit right into the side of her car. She was spun around from the impact. There were many witnesses as it was a crowded corner on a late Sunday morning. Thank goodness the airbags went off and she was protected. She got out of the car a little disorientated. As we had taught her, and as she was insured by my company, Fireman's Fund, she called the phone number supplied to her in case of an accident. Bearing in mind she was standing outside in San Francisco which can be windy, when she was connected she received a voice menu system! She listened to the menu and she had a hard time making it out as it kept cutting in and out because she was on a cell phone in the wind. So she finally gave up. Following this she called me. The first thing she said was: "Daddy I have had a very bad accident but I'm alright." You can imagine the second you hear this your heart starts to pound. "Are you sure you're all right? Are you in a safe place" I asked. She said, "Yes I'm fine, the police officer's coming right now." I said, "Did you call it in?" She said, "I have tried but I'm not sure if there was anybody there, there was a menu and I couldn't make it out." I told her not to worry and that I would deal with it.

When I called the number this is what I heard. "Press one if you have a previous claim. Press two if this is a workman's compensation claim. Press three if this is for Autoglass. Press four if this is a current claim that has not been reported." I pressed four, and then it said "If this is an agent press one. If this is a policyholder press two." I had to pay close attention as it was a little confusing. I finally managed to navigate the system and my daughter was fine. But on reflection later that day I was extremely upset that despite all the work I had done talking about customer focus and the importance of this kind of moment to the customer, this was still happening. My recriminations were also personal because I should have made a call before and checked. I knew that we were probably operating to the traditional physical best practices in the insurance industry, that is, the frequency of the call determines the position it commands on the voicemail.

The people who were working on this had not taken into consideration the emotional nature of the call and the environment the customer would be calling from, like the fact that somebody would probably be calling from a cell phone. I wanted to get this message across about the importance of an emotional Customer Experience to people in Fireman's Fund so I started to play that specific menu to people, describing the story, describing my daughter, the bruises she had, the disorientation; I really created an emotional picture for my employees. I taped the menu and played it that Monday for the 150 people we have as our national leaders group. I was given a commitment that it would change. The next Monday I played it again, it hadn't changed. By the third Monday everything changed, so what I can tell you is it was a great experience for the company, it was a great experience for me, it was extremely important as a watershed event that we're using as a major message to say it's not enough that you think you're there, these are the kinds of tests that tell you if you're there and clearly we weren't close to where we wanted to be. The good news is my daughter is OK and loves her new car!

This is a great story from Chuck that illustrates one of the primary issues that face businesses wanting to improve their experience. Most processes that organizations use are not designed with the customer in mind. In this example, as with many examples we encounter daily when working with clients, the processes were woefully inadequate to address the customer's emotional well-being. In fact it is hard to believe that some processes have not been built in as a deliberate attempt to annoy customers!

In Chuck's case, Fireman's Fund had deployed what they, at the time, considered to be the best practice solution. The problem with best practice is that you may be benchmarking yourself against a low standard, or a "physical" best practice without considering the emotional aspects of the experience. In our experience, organizations fail to put themselves in the shoes of the customer and consider the emotions they will be going through. We are always talking to our clients about the "emotional state" in which customers enter their experience. In this case the emotional state of Chuck's daughter and even himself would have been quite high, and whilst the menu system was efficient, it did not take account of the emotional aspects and the "efficiency" wasn't helpful. Why is this the case? Typically we find little research is carried out on truly understanding customer emotions. There is a wealth of data on the physical aspects of the Customer Experience: how long it takes to answer the call, the average length of the call, and so on, but little on the emotional side.

Having worked with Chuck and the team we know they have the very best interests of the customer at heart and are constantly looking to improve the emotional engagement with customers. I am sure that as you read Chuck's story, you can imagine yourself on that windy corner, desperately trying to navigate a voice menu system, whilst feeling somewhat disorientated by the accident. So why does it take a story like this to galvanize people into action?

Let's let Chuck continue with his observations:

We have people who are linear thinkers, who can get things done, but because they're linear and step by step, they don't leave a path so they don't tend to ask questions that really challenge the thinking. We have abstract thinkers who will sometimes ask all these questions accepting while they have a lot of motion they don't have any movement. The abstract thinker is just essentially going to be chaos because nothing gets done. What I'm trying to do is instil within the Fireman's Fund the whole concept of if we want to innovate and if we want to do things better and if we want to provide on customer focus, which is our major thrust, if we want to be able to do that we have to apply the principle of what are the questions that are critical that we have to find an answer for, as opposed to, we have an answer and we're looking for the question that gives us that answer. When you are dealing with customer emotions it's not necessarily a logical process and therefore it can be counter to how people learn and it's very counter to how most people think.

People need to think about emotions in a different way and, as Chuck suggests, ask different questions. In so doing they will get different answers. To get the most from this new way of thinking, people need to have an insight and understanding of how human beings function, what it is that happens in the brain and how emotions are evoked. Armed with this you will be able to delve deeper into the DNA of the Customer Experience and use this information to better design and genetically engineer the experiences for customers.

In this chapter we will give you a top-level understanding of what is happening in the brain, how people are made up, and how emotions are evoked. At the end of the chapter we'll pull together these threads and use the "so what?" test to explain what this means to the Customer Experience. But just for the moment, sit back and pretend you're back at university. You have a number of lectures to attend today, the first of which is an interesting biology lecture!

What we sometimes fail to realize is that human beings are simply animals who are very intelligent but are still fundamentally driven by emotions. Emotions have evolved over thousands and thousands of years and help us survive as a species. When we feel fear, we enact either "fight or flight." Emotions help us develop long-term strategies without knowing it – for example we fall in love, have companionship, have a sex drive, and experience the desire to produce children to ensure the ongoing existence of the human race. By falling in love we also create a family unit that can work together and protect each member which sustains our species. We form relationships and act in groups as there is safety in numbers, a basic survival technique; we form social groups and crave acceptance in these. Virtually everything we do can be traced back to emotions at the core. How do these emotions get evoked? Well the brain has a lot to do with it. The brain has two main parts, the core and the cortex (Figure 2.1).

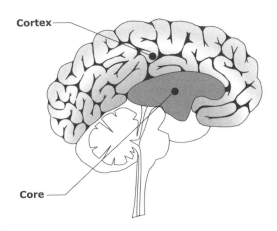

Figure 2.1 The brain

The **core** of the brain is where most of the basic functions reside, that is, our sense of survival, fight or flight, hunger, sex drive, jealousy, and so on. The core is primeval. It makes decisions very quickly but is fairly black and white in its approach. An example of the core in operation is when we find ourselves undertaking tasks without even being aware of what we are doing, or without being aware of having planned them. For instance, our core brain tells us we are angry and before we even realize it we are frowning and clenching our fists. Our core brain tells us we are thirsty and before we know it we have got out of our seat to get a glass of water. Our core helps to assess danger and, for example, can make us move out of the way when we see something dangerous approaching.

The **cortex** is the outer half of the brain and is where the higher functions take place. The cortex is much bigger in humans than in other animals and this is the part that makes us intelligent. The cortex can interpret abstracts, devise strategies and plan. It perceives subtleties, for instance it can interpret people's tone of voice and make an evaluation of what they are really saying by the intonation of their voice. It looks at the relationship among various stimuli, that is, the difference between people's actions and their words. If we perceive a discrepancy, this may indicate to us that the person is lying.

Think about rabbits. They know when they should run and hide, they have sexual desires, they know when to eat, these are all core functions. They do have a cortex, but not a very big one, so they would find it difficult if they were asked to fly a plane! Not least because their feet would not touch the pedals and the headphones would not go over their ears!

Figure 2.2 A strange thought

Now my (poor) attempt at humor and this picture, Figure 2.2, may have been mildly amusing to you. This would have needed help from your cortex to make the interpretation and establish that a rabbit flying a plane is ridiculous, and as such it is funny.

The brain, of course, is a very complex organ and explaining how it works is even more complex. However, for those of us who are non-biology types, let's keep it simple and illustrative. The brain is full of synaptic connections that build pathways for us to pass data, which can be like subroutines to make it easier for us to do things. For instance, as I am typing this book I am thinking about what I am going to write, not which keys I should be hitting. I have built a synaptic pathway in my brain that automatically deals with what keys to hit and therefore allows me to do that automatically and focus on what I am going to write not on the keys. We are born with many synaptic connections, some we use, some die off, some we develop. These connections make our lives easier as we can do things without "thinking" about them. How many times have you driven home without thinking about it and can't remember turning off the freeway. How many times have you been on "automatic pilot" and started to drive into the office when you didn't really mean to go there! These connections make life easy for us, which can be part of the reason why people don't like change. It is easier to carry on doing what you always did as you know what this is, rather than change and do something else that you need to think about.

But how does the brain receive information? This is only achieved through the body, which receives messages through our five senses: touch, taste, sight, sound and smell. Once this information is received, it is transferred to the brain for analysis which may result in the movement of our arm to pick up a flower and smell it. Both the core and the cortex control our motor functions. If we put our hand in a fire then the core will say, remove it! If we are playing a game of tennis our cortex will have a major say in where the best position to place the ball would be.

The core of the brain can inspire the cortex to take action. For example, I am hungry, therefore the cortex works out how I can get food, maybe I am in the forest and I need to construct a trap. When the core and the cortex are in line, decision making is quick, in fact virtually instantaneous. I am cold, I decide to put on a coat; I am scared of this dark alley, I am feeling fear, and so I run out as quickly as I can.

At other times the core and the cortex disagree. You will no doubt have heard the phrase "I am caught in two minds." This can be an indication of conflict between the core and the cortex. Your guts, your "instinct" tells you one thing, which invariably comes from the core, your logic tells you another, which comes from the cortex. For example:

A couple of years ago I took the family to Universal Studios in Florida for the Halloween celebrations. It was great! They deck out the back lot studios in various horror themes like a ghost ship or an old cemetery and so on. As you wander through people jump out at you and scare you. They had axes and chainsaws and so on. As I took my family through, my wife Lorraine and my eldest daughter Coralie, 22, were scared out of their wits! My other two kids, Ben, 20, and Abbie, 17, thought it was great!

Let's think about what is happening here. Logic tells you that Universal

Studios are not in the business of mass murder. Therefore as we entered each scenario I was telling myself this is not real and not to be scared. Clearly I still jumped on a number of occasions as the core forces involuntary actions when confronted with the unexpected but quickly my cortex took over and told me the world was fine. The same applied for Ben and Abbie. The opposite was the case with Lorraine and Coralie. They were so overwhelmed and so scared they could not even look ahead of themselves and were screaming all the time. The cores of their brains were in a major conflict with their cortexes, with their cores clearly winning, as they were on the verge of running out! The fact that Ben, Abbie and I were relatively calm, which was another piece of data for Lorraine and Coralie's cortexes, confused them. It was saying to their cores "Look at them, they are OK, don't be so stupid!" The core says run or fight, the cortex says it's only a game. This conflict therefore causes an emotional response of being confused and feeling unhappy, which is the brain's way of saying this is no fun!

Another example of conflict between the core and the cortex is when you are hungry. Your core may tell you that you are hungry and need to eat but your cortex tells you that you need to lose weight and wants you to stop eating. The result, a conflict and feeling of being unhappy.

Have you unknowingly created a conflict between core and cortex in your Customer Experience? Are you unknowingly creating a conflict between the core and the cortex in your customers and thus causing confusion? Or do you, by luck or judgment, manage to get the core and the cortex in line, thus making decisions quickly as well as delivering a good experience.

But enough of this biology lecture. Let's move away from the brain and change lectures. Let's walk down the corridor to the psychology lecture so we can look at the person in more depth. We walk in when the lecturer is talking about a fundamental motivator for people, "goal states."

Most of us have what are called "goal states." These are the goals we either implicitly or explicitly set for ourselves. For instance, your goal may be "to be happy." The way individuals achieve this may vary enormously. Some people believe that if they earn lots of money they will achieve happiness, others focus on quality of life rather than material goods; others believe a tight family unit will make them happy. Our goal states are the underlying motivation that drives many of our decisions without us even knowing it. If our goal state is happiness and we consider money will give us this, then we will try and get a job that pays the most amount of money; we may also work hard to impress the boss so we can be promoted and get more money. If we think we will be happy by being with the family, we may spend our time resisting jobs that mean we need to work long hours, even if they pay more money. If your goal is to be seen as "successful," then you may like to show people that you are successful by displaying the perceived trappings of success, a big car, designer clothes, a big house, and so on. These goal states are at our core. They are one of the key motivators. If we can understand our customers' goal states, then we can start to design an experience that will appeal to them.

OK, that was the first part of the psychology lecture, now let's look at people's "values."

We are born with a series of inbuilt values, and others we develop over time – some nature and some nurture. On the nurture side, we learn these values from many sources, our parents, our social groups, the culture of the country and society we live in, and so on. An example of a parental value is my parents taught me to be honest and to value this in other people. My friends and my experiences taught me to be streetwise and not take everything at face value. All these values affect the way I now look at the world:

> I was walking around Battery Park in New York City and was approached by a street seller trying to sell me a watch. Good brands at cheap prices. But I did not buy these as I did not trust these people and would be worried that they were not genuine, stolen or would break in a few days. On the other side there were people buying these watches, so they must have considered them a good bargain or worth the risk. This demonstrates again the different values that people have, the different DNA that we need to understand in order to make our experiences most effective.

An example of a social norm is that we would feel embarrassed if our swimsuit came off in the water. Society has dictated that to be naked in public is wrong. In contrast, in some tribes around the world it is normal for women to be topless. In our society this is not the case. When it comes to country cultures I am always fascinated how different countries have different accepted norms. For example:

> It has always surprised my family that when we are in a restaurant in the USA as soon as you have finished your meal, the waiter collects your plates. In the UK the waiter will wait for everyone to finish before collecting the plates. In fact it is considered rude to collect them before everyone has finished. In addition, in the UK we use both our knife and fork together throughout our meal. In the US the norm is to cut the food with a knife and fork and then eat with the fork alone. These examples are not saying the US or UK is wrong, just different.

We are sure that you have different examples from your travels. The implication of this for any multinational organization is they need to understand the different countries' cultures and therefore their citizens' expectations. Thus, when designing a Customer Experience, you need to understand the DNA of that nationality's expectations and not just impose your experience in the host country. A prime example of where this went wrong was Disneyland Paris in the early years. Within Europe the differences in customer expectations are marked. The Customer Experience you receive in France, Italy and Germany is different from how you are treated in the UK. For example:

> In a number of countries in Europe I find the service in general is slow as the culture in the UK is more frantic, particularly in the cities. In Europe they assume that you have plenty of time and don't consider the customer as much as we do in the UK and USA.

In my experience people are less engaging. Another example is Spain where you will find most of the shops shut on Sundays. In Germany, when they applaud a presentation they tend to tap the table as a sign of their appreciation, rather than clap.

The learning for an organization moving into any country is "When in Rome do as the Romans do," as none of these things are wrong, just different. For an organization to provide an effective Customer Experience in each of these countries, they need to understand the DNA of the Customer Experience of that country.

Every day we make decisions on purchases based on emotions and we don't give it a second thought.

People buy emotionally and then justify with logic
(Buck Rodgers, IBM)

Let's stay in the psychology lecture and look at the final subjects that drive our emotional state – traits, moods and emotions (Figure 2.3). To put these quickly into context for you, a trait is something that is inbuilt within you, it is part of your makeup; a mood is a sustained feeling; and an emotion is a feeling which takes place over a short period of time. Let's go into each of these in a bit more depth to understand them further.

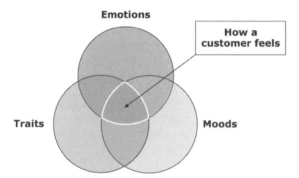

Figure 2.3 The consolidation of how a customer feels

When we look at a person's traits, we are really looking at their makeup. Martin Seligman, in *Authentic Happiness*[1], states that we have a "setting" which is our natural disposition. So some people are naturally happy, some naturally less happy. Think of some of your friends and we are sure you will intuitively recognize this. There are people in our lives who always appear to be happy and cheerful; no matter what life throws at them they respond in a positive manner and always see the "silver lining in every cloud." My wife's Aunt Ena is like this. She is 90, and has lived in Dover, England all her life. In the Second World War she suffered from bombing raids and in more recent years she has lost her husband, her son, and her younger brothers and sisters. Yet when you meet her you are inspired by her zest for life. She acts as if she was 17.

On the other hand, we all know people who are miserable as sin and, not to put too fine a point on it, they are a pain in the neck! Nothing is ever right for them. Everyone else is much luckier than they are. They are similar to Marvin the Paranoid Android from *The Hitchhiker's Guide to the Galaxy*.

The Aunt Ena's of this world look for clues that confirm the world is good and reinforce their naturally happy disposition, that is, the sun is shining, her daughter has called her, her neighbor has popped around for a coffee. She looks for the positive clues that reinforce how she feels. The Marvin the Paranoid Androids look for the bad things that reinforce that the world is against them, that is, it is raining on a day they want to go out, a person they know has a better job than they do, an order has been cancelled and they won't get paid until next month. They believe "bad luck" only happens to them! This doesn't mean that if you are of a happy disposition you will only have good Customer Experiences, but you will be more resilient to their outcomes, that is, if they are frustrating you will know they are frustrating, and while you may never go back there again, it doesn't affect your whole day. If your natural tendency is to be miserable, then the same frustrating experience can reinforce the bad day you are having and you may even get angry in the experience because your threshold is lower.

A friend of mine, Ian Clarke, summed up this key message a number of years ago:

Be careful what you look for, because you will find it.

If you look for things to confirm that you are unlucky, you'll find them. If you look for things to confirm your positive outlook on life, you'll find them too. Therefore if customers feel they are being treated fairly, they will look for other signs that reinforce this. If customers think they are getting bad service, again they look for other signs to confirm this. For example:

> We were on holiday and decided to rent a car to drive around the island and attend a festival in town. We arrived five minutes before 9.30am as prearranged and sat in reception to wait for the car to be delivered. At 10.00am they still had not delivered the car. A prime case of different countries having different norms! It was normal for everyone to be late in this country as it is very laid back. The woman came in at 10.05am and apologized for being late. She could see we were annoyed and frustrated that we had wasted time and wanted to attend a festival in town. The car rental representative then proceeded to tell us about the additional fees we would have to pay, which we had not been previously informed of – a temporary driving license – and an additional insurance fee. As we were already feeling frustrated this just compounded our feelings. Any one of those items individually would not have caused a major headache but it was the combination that caused us the problem.

The same applies to our budget airline experience in Chapter 1. We all know that planes can and do have technical problems, this is not the issue. The issue was when all the problems combined, the incompetence that then occurred, and the manner in which we were treated all heightened our sense of frustration and disappointment.

OK, having dealt with traits, let's look at moods and emotions. A mood is a feeling that lasts for an extended period of time, sometimes days. Clearly you can have a happy mood or a sad mood. You will hear people say "he put them in a mood because ..." and so on. You can look at a mood as being an elongated emotion. Ideally we would put customers in a good mood and this would clearly have a lasting effect.

Emotions are passing feelings. I feel scared, therefore I run away and then after a few minutes I am fine. I feel frustrated when I call the call center and the phone is not answered, but then they answer the phone and I start to forget my frustration. Some people display more emotions than others; you will have heard the phrase "wearing your heart on your sleeve." It is obvious what that person is feeling. Some people tend to become more emotional much quicker than others. For instance, Lorraine (my wife) has a quick temper; I have a very slow temper. However, the reverse is also true for us. Whilst Lorraine gets angry quickly, she is able to forget it much sooner than I can. It takes some time for me to become angry but when I do I remain angry for a lot longer.

There is a constant debate among scholars about the definitions of emotions. For our research we have drawn on some of the leading minds in this field to establish the emotions to research. These are just some of the list of emotions we looked at for our research (Figure 2.4).

We are sure you will agree this is quite a comprehensive list. It is interesting to note that as we feel some of these emotions they can change our body state as well. For example, when we were walking through the scary sets at Universal Studios on Halloween night, the adrenaline was pumping and our senses were heightened. We could hear every little noise, and other people screaming, which made matters worse. As we were scared our body state would have changed. Our heart rate would have increased as blood was pumped through our arteries to get oxygen to the muscles quickly so we could respond to any sudden demands to run away or fight. When you are scared, your body muscles tense and you begin to sweat more.

Think about when you are giving an important presentation; because you are feeling stressed your body state changes. Your hands sweat, your heart races and you have a tendency to speak quickly. Also your mind goes blank as your brain tries to deal with the fear and takes brain capacity away from what you are saying. On the other hand, when you are feeling relaxed your heart rate is slower and you can even fall asleep. Emotions are very powerful and have a direct impact on our bodies.

But how do we know if we have these emotions evoked in us in the first place? Good question. The body takes in data from our five senses: touch, sound, taste, smell and sight. We then appraise that data and make an evaluation. But there is such a wealth of data and sensory input that not all of it makes it through to our conscious state. A great deal of it is dealt with by our subconscious.

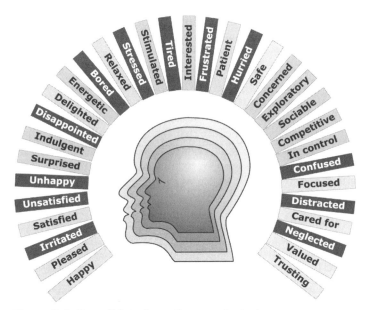

Figure 2.4 Consolidated emotions evaluated

Let me give you an example of this. What is your breathing like? Are you breathing normally? How often are you breathing in and out? Now I have asked you these questions, you are thinking about how you are breathing. Were you breathing beforehand? Of course you were, it's just that this action was being undertaken by your body without you consciously thinking about it. It is only because I pulled this from your subconscious to the conscious that you now notice how you are breathing. If you were to run down the street and started to breathe deeply, you would probably notice your breathing as your body craved more oxygen, your breathing became more strained and you noticed how out of breath you were.

Therefore there are signals that we are receiving every day through our senses, which is the only way we can take information in, that do not register consciously. Think about the last time you watched TV. What were the ads? What were the posters you saw as you drove around yesterday? You would have seen them in your subconscious but not necessarily been conscious of them. If we see the same poster time and time again, eventually they can be raised to our conscious state and we may say: "That poster is up all over the place" or "I saw that same ad on TV last night." If the marketing people have done their targeting properly, then maybe you would see a poster for a Caribbean cruise just at the time you are looking to book a vacation. You have noticed it because this is something you are interested in, your subconscious sees it and allows it to go through the filter into your conscious.

There are lots and lots of messages that the brain takes in about the Customer Experience. What is the quality of the paper the brochure is on? What are the images like? What can I smell? We also associate our senses with situations; the sound of your music can remind you of different moments in your life, and places. The smell of coconut oil reminds us of sunbathing on the beach, the smell of a hospital we associate with being unwell, the smell of popcorn with going to a movie, the smell of baking with a cozy home.

However, given all this knowledge we have, I still find it amazing, in the 21st century, that there is still a great amount of debate about how emotions actually work. The theory currently given the most credence is dual state theory by Damasio, Lange and James. They believe that the following happens when we feel an emotion (Table 2.1).

Table 2.1 Dual state theory

Theory	Explanation
1. We detect sensory stimuli	We smell, see, hear, touch or taste something
2. This stimulus subconsciously activates our body and lower level brain states which, in turn, induces emotional brain and body states	The heart beats faster, the hands sweat, and so on
3. These body/brain states generate a feeling	The feeling is generated
4. At about the same time, we become consciously aware of the feeling	I am feeling cared for, valued, disappointed, scared
5. We then work out why we are feeling this way	I am feeling scared because this is a dark alley and it is late at night
6. We make associations between events/objects in the current situation and what we are feeling	On TV last night I saw that someone was attacked in a similar circumstance
7. We actively organize our memory and learn from what is happening	I should not go down that alley and must not do this again

With this in mind, we need to consider the Customer Experience and realize that we are picking up signals all the time. For instance, your bedroom in the hotel smells a bit strange, you start to look for the reason and see an ashtray or an old banana skin or fungus on the walls. Another example is you may have seen a great ad on the TV of smiling sales assistants in a store but when you visit they are all boring and ignore you.

All these signals we see through our subconscious, which collates them and then, when they reach a threshold, they are raised to our consciousness and for the first time we are aware of them. For example:

We recently went for a drink with a few friends. We walked into a bar, which seemed fine, and sat down. I sat in what I thought was a "comfortable" chair only to find it was as hard as nails. This was my threshold. I then discovered the arms of the chair were all sticky, the table was filthy and the carpet was worn and stained. It didn't take us long to get up and walk out in search of a new venue!

There are hundreds of subconscious signals that organizations are constantly giving to customers which they are not considering. It takes a trained eye to notice these things. Individually, none of these will make a customer say that this was a poor experience but cumulatively they can reach the threshold between subconscious and conscious, making the customer register the poor experience for the first time. One of the most popular services we provide to clients is what we call a "Customer Mirror." This is where we put a mirror up to our clients' own experiences or even their competitors'. Armed with a spy camera, tape recorder and still camera, we record the minute detail of their end-to-end experience, recording the good and not so good signals along the way, which we then play back to the client. Normally our clients are quite surprised by the signals they are giving out and how these can be interpreted by customers. We have completed many interesting experiences, for example traveling on a ferry, visiting electrical stores and even crashing a car and flooding an apartment for an insurance company to test their claims process! For example:

> To test their motor claim procedure, an insurance company gave us a car. We took out their insurance on the car and then crashed it! Crashing a car is not as easy as it sounds, as we obviously didn't want to injure the driver, nor damage the object we were crashing into! So we took it to a forest and found an old tree stump that would do some effective damage to it. When we called the company to report the accident, they sent a tow truck to collect us. All the time we were collating the signals. For instance, when the truck arrived, the driver loaded the car on the truck and informed us he was unable to take us anywhere. He was actually going to leave us in the middle of a forest! Finally he agreed to drive us to an office a few miles away. When we asked for a receipt for the car, he tore a piece of paper from his McDonald's breakfast bag and wrote it on this! During this whole claim process, we spoke with the company on a number of occasions – to deal with car rental while our car was being repaired, to find out how the repairs were going, and so on. Repeatedly they asked for the same information, our name and address, and so on as they were working on different systems. None of this experience individually was bad but the combination made this into a poor experience.

Understanding the detailed signals that your experience is providing to your customers is vital, as their subconscious will be evaluating these and deciding if your experience is good or bad, and raising either of these to their consciousness. Or they are bland and they will forget your experience altogether. Not a good idea when we are in a commoditized market.

OK, the psychology lectures have finished – time for you to collect your thoughts. The next lecture on the Customer Experience is based around a simple question: "So what?" What does all this mean for the Customer Experience? As Chuck mentioned at the beginning, what are the new questions we need to ask ourselves? What does it mean we should do and not do? What are the takeouts? What is the DNA of Customer Experience?

Before we start pulling all this together, I think we should make it clear that sometimes we buy goods that are totally based around the physical aspects of the Customer Experience. For example, it could be that they are just convenient, a taxi waiting outside an airport, a coffee from a street vendor on our way to work. But it could also be that the reason you go to this coffee vendor in the street is that he values you as a customer and always has your cup of coffee waiting for you. Hopefully you can now see the differences between the core and the cortex. In our view you should ideally be trying to align these functions together as best you can, that is, I am hungry and here is a low calorie option I can have even though I am on a diet. I am thirsty and there are plenty of options for me to purchase a drink with a wide variety of flavors. The detail of your Customer Experience is vital as your subconscious will pick up the signals and will bring the poor or good experience to your consciousness.

Your customers are human beings, no matter how sophisticated your products are. I wish I had a dollar for everyone who asked if the principles of the Customer Experience apply in business-to-business (B2B). The answer is yes! The people you are dealing with are human beings and while the products may be of a higher value, and the sales cycle may be drawn out for five years, they still end up picking up signals, appraising those signals and having emotions. I was speaking to a client the other day whose airline has ordered the new Airbus which has been delayed. Are they frustrated? Of course! Are they disappointed? Of course! They are human beings with emotions!

We hope you now realize that your customers have "goal states." If you can uncover what these are, you can provide your customers with a better experience. We understand that asking a customer "could you tell me what your goal states are?," or "what emotions would you like us to evoke in you today?" are not questions most people will be able to answer. Like Chuck says, it's about the questions you ask and the way you ask them. We look at this as peeling back an onion. You need to be skilled at asking the right questions to peel back the onion and get into the core of how a customer is feeling. Over the years we have developed methodologies with lots of psychological inputs to achieve this. It must be said it's not easy but well worth the effort when you can do this. Once you have unlocked the power of this, you will find that it is an incredible financial benefit, as we will discover in the next chapters.

Simon Fox, MD of Comet, one of the largest electrical stores in the UK says:

> Working with Beyond Philosophy we set out to really understand the experience that the customer went through when buying electricals. What emotions do they come into the store with? We walked through every step of the buying journey, step by step. And we did that hundreds of times, sometimes thousands of times and broke the shopping journey down into its constituent parts. We found customers feel very alone, very confused when trying to choose a product, there is nobody they can turn to, no one they could really trust, in this complex world.

We hope you understand that your customers will have different traits, some will be naturally happy, some naturally unhappy and all shades of gray in between. This clearly affects the way they interact with your company. If you can understand the mood your customer is in through their behavior, and so on, you will stand a better chance of creating a great experience. The mood your customers are in when they enter your experience will also affect how they perceive it. If they are in a bad mood, they will look for things to reinforce their bad mood and can thus be very critical of even the smallest thing that goes wrong and then blow this out of proportion. If they were in a happy mood, then they wouldn't even notice it. Again understanding people's emotional state entering the Customer Experience is vital. Here is Simon talking about how they deliver the products to clients. Just imagine you have bought a new high definition flat-screen TV and you are waiting for delivery:

> We did describe it as a Father Christmas moment. It's a happy moment as the product you have been waiting for has turned up but nonetheless a moment fraught with problems if you don't design it and think it through from a customer's emotional perspective.

You see even in the delivery of a TV, surprise surprise, customers have emotions. The reality is that you are evoking emotions in customers every day, but the issue is that you are probably not doing this deliberately and you are not in control. When we start talking with clients about how to deliberately evoke emotions, we normally see people's brows furrow and you can read in their minds that they think this is going to be complicated. Yet we plan to evoke emotions every day but we do it so naturally that we are not aware of it. For some reason we haven't taken this into the business world. For example, have you ever:

- Put soft music on, lit candles or set the lighting level low? Bought your loved one a bunch of flowers or a bottle of their favorite drink? We are sure you have. You are trying to create a mood where they feel loved, cared for and valued.
- Written someone a note just to say that you love them, or a thank you note to say that you are grateful for what they have done for you?
- Bought a birthday or Christmas card to show someone that you still care for them?
- Gone into your kid's bedroom and comforted them after they have had a nightmare, maybe speaking softly to them, hugging them, been reassuring, and turned a night-light on? You are trying to evoke feelings of safety, being cared for, being loved.

On the other side, with a Customer Experience, have you ever:

- Gone into a shop and been totally ignored by an assistant, evoking feelings of disappointment, frustration, neglect?
- Been talking to an account manager and been informed that the vital item you have ordered for your urgent project has been delayed for three weeks, thus evoking feelings of disappointment and dissatisfaction?
- Been greeted at the hotel where you are staying by the receptionist who recognizes you, which then evokes feelings of being valued, cared for and, overall, pleasure?

Of course you have, these things happen regularly. You evoke emotions and emotions are evoked in you every day but they are not normally in your state of awareness.

Now consider if your partner was in bad mood when they came in, only then to see the trouble you had taken to create a lovely meal, would that mellow them, maybe even get them out of their bad mood? The same can be done with a Customer Experience. The customer may enter the experience feeling down but leave feeling great!

Over to Maxine Clark, CEO Build-A-Bear Workshop:

> We wanted our experience to be bright, cheery so even if you were in the mall and needed a quick "pick up" you don't even have to spend any money, just come by and say "Hi" to us and get stimulated and energized.

So now we have understood what is happening with emotions, we can start to look at the DNA of the Customer Experience in more depth.

As we started with Chuck's story, it seems appropriate that we leave with Chuck's thoughts:

> We want to provide great service and somebody says "well the traditional method by which you'll have the most efficient and best service is you'll organize your call menu to offer the most frequent calling type of customer first." On the surface that sounds very logical and is the answer an expert would have given. On the flip side, if they had asked the right questions to identify the emotions we want to evoke, what would be the best service to provide for somebody when they've just got hit in the car. How would we provide the best experience for that person in that extreme moment of stress? So it's about trying to teach people to ask the right questions and then find the right answer.

To build a great Customer Experience we need to think about things in a different way. We need to consider all the above and then we can start to really create a deliberate Customer Experience that will generate dollars. We will be able to focus on evoking the emotions that drive value and eliminate the emotions that destroy value. To achieve this you need to understand that customers have goal states, values, traits, moods and emotions – all the things we have discussed in this chapter. Therefore there are a number of things that will affect your Customer Experience before the customer has even begun dealing with you. So in the next chapter, we look at the emotional state of customers entering your Customer Experience and how this state affects that experience, and, more importantly, what you can do about it.

Note

1. *Authentic Happiness*, M.E.P. Seligman (2002) Free Press, New York.

3 The Importance of the Pre- and Post-Customer Experience

We had been engaged by a bank in the US who asked us to redesign their loan experience in the branch. For us to be effective it is important that we understand where the experience actually begins and ends. In 95% of cases, we find this is different from where the client originally thinks. This client was no different, they had asked us to consider the experience from the moment the customer walked into the branch, whereas our view was that it started well before and continued well after leaving.

Over the years, we have also discovered that to design a great Customer Experience, it is critical to understand the customer's emotional state on entering the experience. Debating this with our client, they agreed and so we conducted some customer research and videoed interactions, walked the experience and conducted interviews with customers in the branch to establish their emotions when they entered the experience. This provided us with valuable insights. We discovered the following:

- Younger people were nervous about asking for a loan. When asked how they were feeling before they entered the branch, they revealed: "It felt like I was going to see the principal (head master). I felt like I had done something wrong." This group of customers tried to do as much as they could on the Web. But when asking for a secured loan, they needed to be interviewed and sign papers, and so on. When entering the experience, this group felt inferior and concerned. We called this group the *principal's office*.
- Older people, felt embarrassed walking into the branch. They had been brought up with the belief that you shouldn't borrow money, that you should "pay your way." Taking a loan was going against their upbringing. We noted that this age group clearly felt they had to fully justify why they needed the money. It was as if they needed to "confess" their sins. These people came into the experience feeling embarrassed and disappointed (with themselves). We called this group *dignity*.
- We also found a group of people who were very confident and knowledgeable when asking for a loan, typically 30–50 years old. These people had loans before with other lenders. They were sophisticated buyers. They came into the experience feeling confident and assured and wanted to get this done as quickly as possible. They had done their homework. The issue was that about 15% of these people knew the system so well that they knew how to manipulate the process but they also had the potential for being poor payers. These we called *sophisticates*.

When we looked at the "in branch" experience, the current process was to

33

invite the customers into the branch. On arrival, they were asked to sit in a waiting area until they were interviewed. Incidentally, we pointed out that even this word "interview" had poor connotations and a word like "consultation" would be more appropriate. The waiting areas in the branches were typically open areas located in full view of all the customers. Without the bank knowing it, the waiting area was having a different effect on each group as their emotional states on walking into the experience were different.

For the *principal's office* group who walked in feeling inferior and concerned, sitting and waiting just confirmed they were going to see the principal! The hidden cameras revealed them fidgeting and sitting on the edge of their chair. We also discovered that the longer they were kept waiting, the greater the strength of feeling of inferiority and the greater their concern was raised.

For the *dignity* group, again the video revealed something interesting. As this group was already feeling embarrassed and disappointed, locating the waiting area in the main branch thoroughfare and asking them to sit where everyone could see them just added to their discomfort. For instance, we discovered they would be worried if a friend saw them and asked why they were at the bank. The last thing they wanted to admit was that they were seeking a loan. The video revealed further interesting behavior. These people tended to sit with their backs to the branch and "hide" so they couldn't be seen by other customers. In one of the branches, a favorite waiting area was behind a large plant that had a chair next to it, a perfect hiding place which provided some privacy. Again, any extended waiting time compounded this group's embarrassment and thus prolonged the agony.

For the *sophisticates* group who entered feeling confident and assured, they thought the whole process was a waste of time. They knew exactly what to do. Their overriding feeling in the branch was one of frustration, they just wanted to get on with it! We could have called this group "the prowlers" as about 65% of them didn't sit, they prowled around, waiting to be called in so they could leave and get on with something more productive.

Without looking at the emotions evoked on entering the experience, none of this would have been revealed. Our recommendations were to alter the experience for each of these groups. There were some common aspects that would help all these groups in different ways. For different reasons all the groups wanted to be seen quickly, therefore a more efficient appointment system was implemented. Now when the customer arrives, the branch manages their resources and appointment times so well that customers are led straight into a consultation room, with no waiting, no fear of being seen by other customers, or feeling they were outside the principal's office. This aspect of the experience has now become one of the key performance indicators for the branch. We also trained all the branch staff on the characteristics of the groups and explained how to identify them. To get the message over of the way customers felt, as part of the training we implemented a simulation game that was set in a classroom at school. When the branch delegates did something wrong, they had to sit outside the principal's office. When they did this, we asked them how they felt. They used the same words that the principal's office group used. With this kind of experiential learning, they quickly understood and could relate to how customers must be feeling on entering the experience. Where possible, we also "generation matched." That is: we tried to ensure that younger people were interviewed by the younger employees in the branch.

For the principal's office group, at the beginning of their consultation we proposed that they were put at their ease by the branch people not sitting behind desks. We also ensured they spent time in small talk, explaining what was going to happen, and calling them by their first name.

For the dignity group, we allowed a longer period of time for their "confession." We had discovered this was a cathartic experience for this group. The statistics showed us that if we did not do this, they would exit the experience with this burden still on their shoulders and would consider this a poor experience. We also moved the waiting areas into a more secluded place. We found that it was also important for the dignity group that the person interviewing them was not a young male, as they were seen to be judgmental.

For the sophisticates we speeded up the process. We also enhanced the checks to ensure they were not bad payers. No time was wasted at the beginning of the interview on settling them down. It was very business like and efficient as this was what would make this group happy.

The result of all this work? Loan conversions increased by 17%.

Understanding the emotional state of the customer pre and post your experience can be vital to how effective the experience is and how much the financial gain will be.

But how is this "emotional state" generated? Over the years, we have discovered a number of stages that an organization needs to consider. As we learned in the last chapter, it can be the person's traits that affect the experience. For some it can be life experience or everyday occurrences like arguing with your boss or feeling tired that affect the experience. Alternatively, it can be something directly caused by that experience. These are feelings a customer would not have felt if they were not going to participate in your experience.

We have categorized these stages as follows: traits, life events, pre-experience, the experience, and post-experience.

Traits – As we now know, traits are what you are born with. Also included here are the nurture aspects of your life, that is, your upbringing, your country's culture and so on.

Life events – These are things that happen to you in life that affect the Customer Experience. For example, you may have just had an argument with your partner and are in a bad mood. You may have just been promoted at work and are in a good mood. Maybe it's your birthday, your anniversary or you have a bad cold. Maybe you have just had a car accident and are feeling rattled or upset. All these things will affect the emotional state on entering the Customer Experience. Here we also include being in a mood, as the output of these life events can "put you in a mood," which then carries into the experience and affects your perception of it. People in a bad mood will subconsciously look for things that support the notion that this is a poor experience.

These moods are nothing to do with the experience but clearly can affect how the customer enters your Experience and therefore have a major affect on its outcome.

Pre-experience – These are influences outside the actual experience but are as a direct result of wanting or needing to take part in that experience. A good example of this is the Memorial Hermann Hospital System, in Houston, Texas, which we discuss in Chapter 8. We were asked to redesign their cancer experience. It is difficult to think of a more emotional experience than this. Clearly, the emotional state of a person going in to see the physician/doctor and then visiting the hospital for tests and treatment is fundamental. With this in mind we conducted research with cancer patients. To our surprise one of the key issues they faced had nothing to do with the cancer, as the hospital and their family group were already dealing with this very well. One of their big issues was traffic. The traffic in Houston is terrible! Therefore, when they were visiting the hospital for treatment on a regular basis, it was taking some time to get there and this was causing stress and tiredness before and after treatment, adding to an already difficult experience. In the redesign of this experience, they took this into account and considered ways to address this issue, short of building more roads! The great news is this project has been so successful it led to the winning of the most prestigious system-wide internal award.

The experience – This is the actual Customer Experience. Clearly, this is totally within your control. In our view, you also need to consider any outside influences that are brought into your experience like parents shopping with screaming children, or a bored partner in a woman's clothes shop. A number of organizations have already begun to tackle this by offering crèche facilities, seating with newspapers for bored partners, and so on.

Post-experience – What happens after your experience? Where does it stop? Again, a subject often missed. The delivery of products and services, the ongoing use of a service, electricity or a telephone, the way user manuals are written, the after-sales service or lack of it should all be considered as part of the whole customer experience.

For example, in the B2B world, it is quite common for the salesperson to be very interested until the point that you have bought their service from them and then you do not see them again, sometimes called "hit and run." A further example is rental vacation homes and villas. It amazes us how you are always provided with the directions to travel to the villa but never for the return journey. Whilst you can clearly reverse the route, this is not always clear or convenient. We believe it shows a mindset that considers the experience has finished as soon as the customer has left the property, when, clearly, if they get lost and miss their flight, this reflects on the whole experience which ends up being poor.

After the experience, it is also vital for the organization to consider "buyer's remorse." This quite common concept is when a customer questions whether the purchase they have made is the right one. For example:

Lorraine and I were shopping for jewelry to celebrate our 25th wedding anniversary. After a great deal of deliberation, Lorraine decided on a necklace. As there was quite a wide selection, Lorraine was uncertain if she had made the right choice and suffered from buyer's remorse for the next few days. Should she have chosen the other necklace with the heavier chain or the silver as opposed to the gold one?

These emotions of doubt and insecurity can lead customers to take things back and thus impose a cost on the business. Organizations need to consider how they deal with the post-experience and define where the end of the experience is.

Without knowing it, a great deal of the post-experience contact is made via market research. We have all received a call or letter asking us to complete a 10-minute survey. Market research is part of the Customer Experience. It tells your customers subconsciously what you are interested in. Also what happens or doesn't happen with the results of these surveys speaks volumes about the organization. For example, do you follow up on the customers who have given you a poor rating and inform them of the actions your organization is going to take to put things right? Or do you do what most organizations do, simply compile the data, create a report and ignore the customers who have taken part, especially those who have given you poor feedback? What do you think these people now think of your organization? Has their perception improved or remained the same? This action tells them subconsciously they are not important.

You may be saying this is all very interesting but so what? What do you expect me to do if the person has just had an argument with their partner? Well, you can take that view, or you can see it as an opportunity to improve your Customer Experience. The attitude that all this is too hard will be taken by a number of your competitors. We are not saying this is easy, it's not. It takes a bit of lateral thinking and some hard work. However, a number of our clients bear testimony to how well this works, and demonstrate that it can be done.

For example, Simon Fox, MD at Comet, speaks on how he and the team began to understand what the customer was feeling before and after the experience:

We also undertook quite a significant amount of research into what people felt about our Customer Experience. We discovered that customers thought we had good prices, good ranges, but overall the impression of the brand was not what we wanted because we were not delivering a consistently good experience.

We described it as a valley of despair. This is where customers anticipated the excitement of owning the appliance, they enjoyed the appliance when they got it home, but the whole process of buying it was the low point in the valley, in their shopping experience.

Now they understood this, they could do something about it. Previously they had not extended their thoughts into this space. Our experience shows that the further you can reach back into your customers' lives to understand them and their emotional state, the better you will be able to provide a great Customer Experience. With that knowledge, the minimum we would recommend you do is to brief your employees on the findings and ask them to be empathetic when they encounter these situations. What we would like to see you do is to design your experience with this information in mind and make allowances for the emotional state of the customer entering the experience. For example:

> When we arrived on holiday in Antigua it was very hot and after traveling for over nine hours, we were tired. On arrival at the hotel we were shown to some comfortable armchairs and the registration was completed there rather than standing at reception. We were also given a complimentary cold drink and cold hand towel to cool us down. They had considered the emotional and physical state in which we would arrive.

Experience extension is a concept where an organization decides to extend and take control of some external factors, normally deemed outside their direct Customer Experience (Figure 3.1).

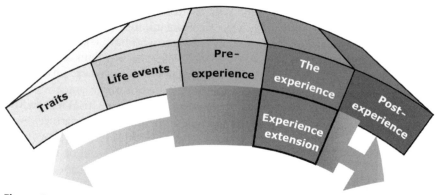

Figure 3.1 Experience extension

An example of this is courtesy buses for hotels to and from airports. Prior to this customers had to find their own way to the hotel. These organizations realized this was a problem for the customer, potentially resulting in them going somewhere more convenient. Many have now extended their pre- and post-experience by collecting and returning guests to airports. Virgin Atlantic and a few other carriers now offer a limousine service to pick you up and take you to the airport and then take you to your destination on the other side, extending their experience both ways.

To start to put this all together and redesign a Customer Experience, in our view you need to be able to answer one simple question:

What is the Customer Experience you are trying to deliver?

In our experience most organizations cannot answer this question. We covered this in our previous books so we will not go through it again here, but essentially this is a clear articulation of the experience you are trying to deliver and includes physical and emotional words. This should be expressed in what we call a "Customer Experience Statement," a clearly defined and practical description that everyone should be able to understand. Now we know the emotions that drive and destroy value, we would recommend that these emotions are considered for inclusion in your statement or are mapped into that experience. This is the path Mark Gater, Customer Experience program manager at Britannia Building Society, led his team down. Mark explains what they did:

> Our question was, "What was that Customer Experience going to be?" In addition and equally important, what was it going to take to move us from where we were to where we wanted to be, delivering a deliberate experience every time. We gradually got our head around the fact that for us it was largely going to be based on emotions and the feeling we were going to evoke in customers. I have to say this was a shock to me. This was a huge change in our approach.
>
> We decided which emotions we wanted to evoke by drawing on a pile of internal research, best practice research and, importantly, customer research. We started to hone down the possible emotions. Over a period of time we got down to the five that we ended up with. They map quite well onto the emotions you are discussing in the book.

If you haven't read our previous books, we would encourage you to particularly look at our Moment Mapping® methodology[1]. This is our process for redesigning a Customer Experience but also, importantly, incorporating emotions into its delivery to create a deliberate, consistent Customer Experience. Simon Fox, MD at Comet, explains how they have used this:

> What was very helpful was following the Moment Mapping® process which really made us understand every step of the journey; in our case the decision to buy a television, from the pre-research, to entering the store, to orientation and then, critically, a conversation with the sales colleague. The customer journey is a complex one of orientation of the store, browsing on one's own, narrowing the selection down, entering into a dialogue, choosing a product, buying it and having it delivered and indeed fixing it if it goes wrong.
>
> The process we went through was to split the journey down into twelve individual elements, understand those elements in detail and then put together a series of very concrete actions. There are certain things that you should definitely do and things you should definitely NOT do in each of those twelve steps. These "dos and don'ts" have absolutely been taken on board and are now ingrained in our operating model for in-store procedures. So there's nothing loose about this, retailers have to have hard concrete procedures. What we have done, I believe, is make the delivery of an experience a consistent process that happens every time.

Let us assume that you now have your Customer Experience Statement and you know the emotions that you are trying to evoke. You understand the customer emotions coming into the experience and you have extended your experience with some innovative thinking. You are now redesigning your Customer Experience, maybe using Moment Mapping®. A key part of redesigning your experience is to consider the "peak end rule."[2]

According to the peak end rule, we judge our past experiences almost entirely on how they were at their *peak* (either pleasant or unpleasant) and how they ended. Virtually all other information appears to be discarded, including net pleasantness or unpleasantness and how long the experience lasted.

> In one experiment, one group of people were subjected to loud, painful noises. In a second group, subjects were exposed to the same loud, painful noises as the first group, after which followed somewhat less painful noises. This second group rated the experience of listening to the noises as much less unpleasant than the first group, despite having been subjected to more discomfort than the first group, as they experienced the same initial duration, and then an extended duration of reduced unpleasantness.[3]

Here is another example of the peak end rule:

> We were working for a client in the mobile (cell) phone sector and had been asked to look at contract renewals. We decided to test the process and phoned the contact center to complete a renewal. We entered into a long discussion with the agent about which phone and tariff would be most suitable for our usage. He suggested one tariff. As we had done our homework on what the competition was offering, we challenged him on the rates he proposed and pushed for a further discount, which was forthcoming. In fact, as we continued to press him for more and more discount he gave way. He clearly needed the deal! At the end of the call the overall feeling was, on the one hand, pleasure that we had a great deal; on the other hand, disappointment that the company had tried to overcharge us, by not giving us the best deal in the first place. If we hadn't been persistent, we would be paying additional money. The peak emotion was success, the end emotion was resentment.

Another example:

> What do you remember about the 2006 World Cup soccer final? Probably the peak emotion you felt was surprise when the Frenchman, Zinedine Zidane, one of the world's greatest players, head-butted his Italian opponent and was then sent off. The end emotion was the drama of the penalty shoot-out.

In designing an experience, we believe that it is imperative you take these emotions into account.

To summarize, it is important that you understand the customer's emotional state coming into the experience, ideally you will reach back into their lives and understand what they are like and then customize your experience to evoke the emotions that drive value. If it provides you with benefit, you can look to extend your experience, either backwards or forwards. Either way you will want to avoid evoking the emotions that destroy value. These destroyers of value are what we will look at next.

Notes

1. Moment Mapping® is a methodology to design an emotionally engaging Customer Experience. This is outlined in *Building Great Customer Experiences*, C. Shaw and J. Iven (2004) Basingstoke, Palgrave Macmillan, or on our website at www.beyondphilosophy.com.
2. *Well-being: The Foundations of Hedonic Psychology*, D. Kahneman, E. Diener and N. Schwarz (1999) Russell Sage Foundation, New York.
3. Wikipedia.

4   The Destroying Cluster

We were running a series of 15 executive educational events for one of the world's leading banks, using a four-star hotel in central London. I was the opening speaker on the first day. After the second event, we noticed a number of delegates were arriving late for the opening. Upon investigation, it was due to the poor service at breakfast. So the following day I decided to investigate.

On arrival at the restaurant, I was confronted by a sizable line of about 15 people, waiting patiently to be seated. Ahead of me I could see plenty of empty tables, so the reason for the line was a bit puzzling. I waited about 15 minutes to get to the head of the line. By this time I was feeling "hurried" and "frustrated" as I hadn't allowed for this delay, knowing it was a self-service buffet and therefore normally quite quick. I certainly wasn't going to have time for the relaxing breakfast I was hoping for. When I got to the head of the line I was greeted by the maître d' who asked my room number, looked down a long list of names and numbers, crossed off my name and showed me to one of the many empty tables before going back and repeating the same process with the next guest.

So what was the problem here? Some would say it was the process and it needed changing. I would agree, but to stop there is only to look at the problem from a superficial level and does not reveal the root cause. To do this we need to look at the DNA of this Customer Experience. I would like you to consider two questions.

Q: Why did the hotel insist that the maître d' checked everyone's room numbers before sitting them down?

A: Quite obvious really. The hotel thought they would lose money because not all the guests would pay for breakfast. While there are a number of ways this could have been handled, this is the process the hotel chose. However, the root cause is that the hotel does not trust their guests and they had not considered the impact of this process on the guests, or they had but their mistrust of the guests outweighs their concern.

Q: Why did they not provide the maître d' with someone to assist him during peak times as this was when the problem occurred? If someone escorted guests to their table, the process would be two or three times quicker. Why wasn't this done?

A: Again a simple answer. It would cost more money to have someone for the breakfast period to undertake this task. When it comes down to it, the customer's experience and their feelings are not important enough to find a solution to the problem.

The basic issue is:

- Management didn't care enough about the problem to solve it
- They are too internally focused
- They did not bother to think through the consequences of their actions
- They do not care about the customer.

I decided to take the problem up with the manager of the restaurant as it had a knock-on effect for our experience. We were concerned, as stated in the previous chapter, that this was not putting our clients in the right "mood" coming into our event.

Here is the conversation I had with the maître d' and the manager. I have outlined what I was thinking and my interpretation of what they were thinking, given their body language and tone of voice.

Table 4.1 A conversation interpreted

What the person said	What I/they were really thinking
Colin: (to the maître d' when reaching the head of the line) I would like to complain. I have been waiting in line for 15 minutes. There are obviously plenty of empty tables here so why can't I just come in and sit down?	I want to tell them I am upset and feeling irritated.
Maître d': I need to check your room number to see if you need to pay for your breakfast.	I need to answer you but I am far too busy to go through this again.
Colin: I appreciate that, but why can't you do this another way?	I know that but this is silly, surely there is a better way.
Maître d': This is the way we do it.	Doesn't he realize that I know this causes a problem, the longer he keeps me talking, the longer the line gets!
Colin: Can I see the manager please?	I am now starting to feel frustrated that he is not listening to me and his body language supports that … so it's pointless carrying on this conversation.
Maître d': Certainly, he's over there (pointing).	Thank goodness, he's going; I have a big line of people to deal with. Maybe he can talk sense into the manager anyway.
Colin: (to the manager) I wanted to let you know that I have been waiting for 15 minutes to get a table. There are obviously plenty of empty tables, so why can't I just come in and sit down?	I also want you to know I am upset.
Manager: I am very sorry, can I get you a tea or coffee now sir?	I need to acknowledge his complaint (I learned that in training). Maybe I can divert him away from his complaint.

Table 4.1 cont'd

What the person said	What I/they were really thinking
Colin: A coffee please. Are you aware this happens every day? Why do you need to check people's room number at the door? Why don't you let them sit down first and then check their numbers, when you ask them if they would like tea or coffee?	I know you are trying to divert me but it's not going to work. I am sure you have thought of this but here is a practical suggestion.
Manager: We need to ensure that we have everyone's room numbers so we can ensure they pay for their breakfast.	We have already discussed this at a team meeting as we have had other complaints. I just need to get out of this conversation.
Colin: So you don't trust your customers then?	OK he is annoying me now so I will hit him with a blunt question.
Manager: (silence and a look of embarrassment.) We have had some people who don't tell us their numbers.	Oh that's a difficult question to answer. The reality is we don't but I can't say that!
Colin: I appreciate that but surely there is a better way of doing this?	I will try to appeal to his better nature now he is cornered.
Manager: We have just been very busy today, it doesn't normally happen this way.	I will make an excuse so I can get away.
Colin: I am very sorry but it does. I have been here delivering an event in your conference rooms for the last three weeks and it's the same every time.	I am now annoyed that he thinks I am an idiot and I know he is just making an excuse so he can get away.
Manager: Oh (another silence and the face of a little boy who has been found out).	Damn, he has got me!
Colin: I am not sure if you know but we are running a Customer Experience educational event in your conference rooms. Firstly, this process makes everyone late and, secondly, as we are discussing the Customer Experience, everyone is complaining about the poor experience they are receiving at breakfast.	I don't think they understand this is not just about waiting in line for 15 minutes, the repercussions of this are far-reaching: "Post-experience" as outlined in the previous chapter.
Manager: No, I wasn't aware. I am very sorry but there is nothing I can do about it.	I understand what you are saying but there is nothing I can do, so let me be honest with you.
Colin: Can't you just get someone else to help the maître d' seat people? That would speed things up.	Maybe another practical suggestion would work.
Manager: No, I'm sorry, my boss won't give me another person to do this.	I need to be honest, this guy knows what he is talking about.

Table 4.1 cont'd

What the person said	What I/they were really thinking
Colin: Well, please tell your boss that if this continues we will need to look elsewhere as we don't want our delegates to start their experience with us in a bad mood as it affects the whole day.	I am clearly not going to get anywhere here so I'm going to stop hassling him.
Manager: OK I will do.	I am not going to do this as we have had the conversation many times before and the answer is always the same.

Do you know what the tag line of this hotel is?

Beyond Expectations

Breakfast was certainly beyond my expectation! The irony is that this tag line, which was on flip charts and all over the place, irritated me for the rest of the day as it is clearly rubbish.

This typical interaction destroys value. In this example, I felt *frustrated*, *irritated* and *unhappy*. The ultimate result? We moved our business. In fact, what we found was just one of the "inside out" behaviors.[1] Let's also look into the DNA of this Customer Experience in more depth and start to put a value on this.

The business case for change

Given the size of the hotel and the fact that breakfast was included in the rate for most guests, I would guess that there would be, at most, 10 people a day not entitled to breakfast – 10 who took it and ran away. Using central London prices, we have converted to US$ at a rate of $1.80 to £1. This would be:

10 × cost of breakfast £15 ($27) = £150 ($270) per day, £1,050 ($1,890) per week = £54,600 per annum ($98,280)

This is the potential loss of revenue – quite a significant amount for that size of hotel. This is what is driving them to put this process in place. As we indicated in the story, the hotel could have chosen to collect people's details when they ordered tea and coffee, once they had been seated, but I guess the problem with that is it may be a bit more hit and miss, but it would cost less than the £54,600 ($98,280) above.

Another way to solve this problem would be to have a person to escort people to tables; this would typically only be for the two-hour peak period. Let's say we need to pay someone overtime to cover this. Hotel staff are not normally very well paid, so let's call it £8 ($14.40) per hour (minimum wage in the UK is £5.35 ($9.63)). Therefore, two hours at £8 ($14.40) per hour is £16 ($28.80).

Let's round it up for overheads, and so on to £20 ($36) per day; 7 days = £140 ($252) per week = £7,280 ($13,104) per year. This includes weekends when they may not need extra staff as the clientele changes and breakfast times are more spread out.

This is far cheaper than losing £54,600 ($98,280) per year by not having the process and just accepting the loss of 10 breakfasts a day. But we are investing the £7,280 ($13,104) in a person to help the maître d'.

Now let's look on the other side, the revenue. We were spending about £5,940 ($10,692) per event. Therefore, for the remaining 12 events the hotel would have received £71,280 ($128,304).

Therefore, with the worst case scenario of losing the breakfasts against what business they lost from us, they have lost £16,680 ($30,024). Let me stress that is just from us. We haven't included the cost of handling the customer complaints this would cause. There were plenty of other guests in the line saying they were frustrated and wouldn't return. It also forgets all the ill will this one simple policy is causing. Having breakfast is one of the last things you do in a hotel stay, so consider the peak end rule outlined in the last chapter, this could also have an effect. Let us assume that there are another seven organizations over a year that did the same. That would be £116,760 ($210,168).

I wonder how many other individuals refused to go there again because of this. It is typical that time-poor clients are also the high-value ones as well, thus causing more loss of revenue. This is not even looking at the lifetime value! That would be scary! Over 10 years = £1,167,600 ($2,101,680). The short-term loss is bad enough but the longer term loss is even greater.

For a moment, let us take a step back and consider what has happened here. One poorly designed process that evokes feelings from the Destroying Cluster (Figure 4.1) has resulted in a huge loss of revenue. We are sure there are many examples that you know of that are similar. It constantly surprises us that many businesses do not do this simple type of calculation.

We believe the Emotional Signature of Value research has now gone to the next stage of sophistication in being able to understand the financial impact of emotions, as you will see from the case studies at the end of this and the next three chapters.

We cannot say this any more plainly:

Evoking the emotions in the Destroying Cluster costs you money

It costs you money through lost revenues and through additional costs. Here is the irony. Senior business leaders love to talk about numbers, and what they are doing to achieve their revenue, profitability, costs and targets, and yet year on year they are presiding over organizations in which evoking the Destroying Cluster of emotions is endemic. They are costing themselves millions by providing a poor experience. We very much doubt anyone in this hotel went into this calculation that took only 30 minutes to formulate. They don't because they just think of the £54,600 ($98,280) they are potentially losing. They are fixated and blinkered, looking solely from the internal side of the equation and not from the customers' perspective.

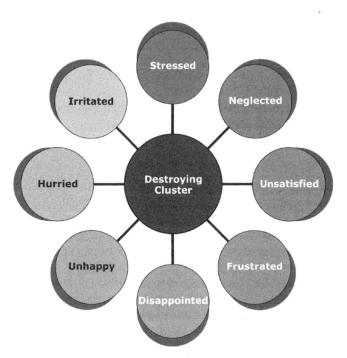

Figure 4.1 Destroying Cluster of emotions

At the same time, these emotions are costing millions in failure costs. Consider how much time is spent on dealing with customer complaints, how many people are involved in it. How much management time is spent on unhappy customers? Consider the time it takes to deal with product returns, disputes over invoices, and so on. All this adds up and should be considered and built into any case for change.

Just to be clear, we are *not* saying that these are the *only* emotions that turn customers off, but these have been shown to be the *only* emotions that are statistically significant and proven to be directly linked to reduction in loyalty and spend. Other emotions such as anger, fury and annoyance are either subsets of the Destroying Cluster or not statistically significant enough to show a direct link to loyalty or spend. However, our experience indicates they would reduce loyalty and spend.

We are sure that you are starting to realize that emotions are not as straightforward as dealing with physical aspects of the experience, such as delivery times, opening hours or average call handling times. That is why many organizations choose not to become involved and, again, therein lies your opportunity.

It is important to remember that the emotions within each cluster interact with each other and can be linked (Figure 4.2). For instance, you may be feeling *frustrated* within an experience that then leads you to feeling *stressed*. Alternatively, you may feel *hurried* or *neglected* which leads you to being *disappointed*. Therefore, if you improve your processes so that customers feel less *hurried*, this can lessen the *stress* a customer is feeling and the *neglect* and *disappointment* they may feel with the experience. By addressing one emotion, this can be linked to other emotions, thus they can have a knock-on effect to other emotions; they can be interrelated. It is about understanding the DNA of what is happening within your experience. If you are not evoking any or many of these emotions, great! It is imperative that you consider what emotions you are evoking now, as this can act as an early warning system of the build-up of emotions in the Destroying Cluster. Once we know the emotions you are evoking, we can identify the root causes and put in solutions to solve them.

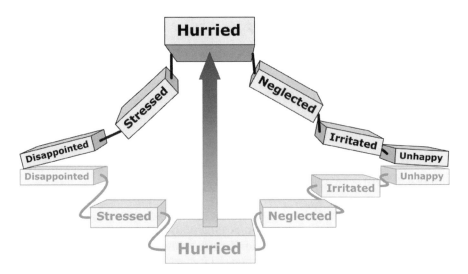

Figure 4.2 Interrelationship of emotions in a cluster

You will see in Figure 4.3 that all these emotions can be correlated. The arrows point from one emotion that can affect another emotion. For instance, if you are feeling *stressed*, it may be because you are feeling *neglected, unhappy,* or *frustrated*, and so on. These emotions interrelate and can be linked.

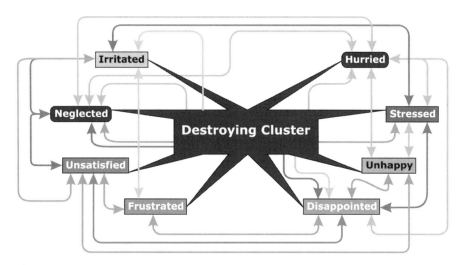

Figure 4.3 Correlations between emotions

Let us give you an example:

We were working with an airline client in the US who had been using our Emotional Signature measurement tool to monitor their Customer Experience every few months. We noticed there was a steady increase in feelings of neglect felt by their frequent fliers. On closer investigation we discovered that during this period their marketing department had stopped offering their frequent fliers exclusive special offers. They had also moved to a self-service operation and thus the human contact the passenger had with check-in employees was no longer encouraged. In delving down into the DNA of this, we discovered the combination of activity had not been coordinated and had led to the overall increase in the "neglect" score.

In undertaking the investigation, we found that having more people to provide assistance in the self-service check-in areas dedicated to their frequent flier members not only pulled back the scores of neglect but also improved scores of "unsatisfied" and "disappointed." In addition, some of the exclusive offers were reinstated as well as a relaunch of all the other benefits that a frequent flier enjoys, as we discovered a number of these benefits were not realized by the customer. This raised the score back to its original position.

In short, you need a method to measure and monitor the emotional engagement of your customers that truly understands the emotions they are feeling.

The key issue is to identify what emotions you are evoking in your experience and to what degree. To do this is not easy. You can imagine just walking up to a customer and saying, "Good morning, what emotion have we just evoked in you?" Firstly, this is not something that customers normally consider. Secondly, they are not very good at identifying the real emotions they are feeling. Typically, what they say is quite superficial. Therefore, we would recommend that you go through a process of peeling back the onion, that is, going through different layers to get to the core, the actual emotions. With some psychological input, we have created a process that truly achieves this. Let us stress this is not something you should undertake lightly and we would recommend that you might want some expert help as you are now playing with people's minds and their inner thoughts.

Once this is achieved, training your team is essential. In the frontline training we undertake for clients we always try to make the training as real as possible, by making live calls or taking people out on "safari" into shopping centers to give them real experiences. Neville Richardson, CEO of Britannia, gives an excellent example of how they communicated what the Customer Experience is about for their employees:

> We undertook road shows around the business about 18 months ago to every single member of staff. We focused on improving the awareness of what we actually meant by the customer experience. We used a great video of a staged experience of one of our board members, Phil. The group executive board had all gone for a meal one evening but what Phil didn't know was that the waiters were actors and we had placed hidden cameras in the ceiling and the flowers in order to capture this experience! Everything that happened to Phil was orchestrated to go wrong. You would visibly see the emotions rising in him and see him getting more and more frustrated, irritated and disappointed as the evening wore on. For the road shows we then overlaid a commentary based around the Customer Experience we are trying to deliver. For instance, as they saw Phil getting annoyed, the commentary said "Do you think Phil feels 'in control' at this point? Is he feeling 'understood' when he orders his favourite beer and the waiter comes back with a coke?" We showed this to 3,500 people! So in a very light way, we introduced the Customer Experience and emotions with that. You're actually talking to people about emotions in a very professional way and letting them have a good laugh about something that probably sticks with them. It also shows them how negative emotions can destroy a Customer Experience.

The training of frontline people is fundamental to any successful program. But before we get on to the case study, let us look at each of the Destroying Cluster of emotions in turn, offer you a definition and some practical examples of situations where these emotions are evoked and what you could do about it.

Stressed

Definition: A feeling of being overloaded, not feeling in control, trying to undertake too many actions at the same time, being put under stress by someone or something. Capable of affecting physical health, usually characterized by increased heart rate, a rise in blood pressure, muscular tension, irritability.

When someone is feeling stressed during an experience, it can have a hugely detrimental effect on the organization. When you are stressed, you are worried, concerned, everything you experience is heightened and potentially exaggerated in importance; people who are stressed tend to be unreasonable and overreact to even the smallest mistake.

For example, while working with one of our banking clients in the US, we discovered, using the Emotional Signature, they were causing their mortgage customers stress. Looking into their DNA, we discovered this was primarily when the customer came into the branch to sign the paperwork for a mortgage. We discovered there were a number of inaccuracies in the paperwork, which not only caused an abortive visit for the customer but also this potentially delayed the purchase of the house. We all know that house moves are one of the most stressful life events. This added to the stress and caused further delays. On looking at the DNA of this experience, we discovered the back office employees were targeted on speed, not accuracy, and therefore had to get as many applications sent to branches as quickly as possible; the fact that these were inaccurate was less important. Clearly, a ridiculous practice but not noticed until we looked at why these customers were feeling stressed.

Simon Fox, MD at Comet, gives us a good example of how customers can feel stressed, and other emotional triggers their research uncovered:

> The research showed that emotionally customers were stressed that the delivery wouldn't turn up and we discovered it was a relief to know the goods were there. The research uncovered other emotional triggers, for instance when the customer realizes two delivery people were going to have to walk through their home, carrying a large appliance and therefore there was potential to damage the home. Another one was that it might be raining and will they bring mud onto the new carpet, or will the appliance actually work? There are many, many emotions that you discuss in this book.

The typical causes of stress are:

- Something is not delivered or provided to a customer in a timely, accurate or complete manner
- The process takes a lot longer than the customer expected
- The customer is dependent on this item or service for an important life event
- A customer is severely let down
- The customer is in a hurry and there are assistants doing nothing when they could be reducing the size of the line
- It is difficult to find the right person to talk to
- Customers cannot locate the items that they require
- Customers' questions are not answered
- Goods are delivered late.

An everyday story of stress in an experience

A B2B client is attending an important presentation by a supplier at their premises. The client is naturally a highly strung person (one of their traits as we discussed in Chapter 2). The client underestimated the traffic to the supplier's office, she is now late for the presentation and, as if this is not enough, on arrival, she cannot find a parking space. As you can imagine, she is now entering the Customer Experience feeling stressed. Fifteen minutes into the presentation, the bulb in the projector blows and they spend 10 minutes searching for a new one. The client has a deadline to leave the presentation as she is meeting her boss who wants an update on this project. She is worried she will have to leave the presentation before it is finished and will not have the answer that her boss is looking for, and he's not renowned for his tolerance.

What could be done to relieve the stress of this client?

The account manager should have built a good relationship with the client and understood her emotional predisposition. The supplier should have thought to inform the client of the traffic conditions and given her advice on travel times or offered to inform her of a nearby hotel (experience extension). A parking space should have been reserved for the client. A backup bulb or projector should have been present. For the "post-experience," the supplier should have advised the client of the time it would take to travel to her meeting and have prepared a report that the client could take or give to her boss to answer some of the questions he might have. All these actions would have reduced the stress of this event.

Neglected

Definition: To be paid little or no attention to; fail to take heed of someone's comments/presence; treating them with disregard; failing to care for a person, failing to look after someone's property or well-being.

When you neglect someone, you are really saying they are not important. This can be done by what you say or do, or perhaps more significantly by what you don't say or do. Maslow's hierarchy of needs tells us that one of the basic human needs is to be part of a group, to be recognized and accepted. Customers who are neglected feel they are being ignored and can feel abandoned. This is certainly not a way to gain loyal customers!

For example, a B2B client of ours in the construction industry discovered they did not have one customer for a job, they actually had four groups of customers: the client, architects, consultants, and mechanical and engineering. Typically, the client would commission the architect or consultant to manage the project. Balancing attention to all these customers was a challenge to ensure no one felt neglected. In some cases, the architects and the consultants were worried that the construction company would neglect them and go straight to the client, thus eliminating them. The construction company therefore went out of their way to ensure they were not neglecting any of these customer groups.

The typical causes of neglect are:

- Ignoring a customer
- Losing customer details and asking them to provide them again
- Asking the customer to repeat information already provided
- Not training staff to pay attention when the customer comes into your experience
- Not answering the phone
- Not including all the customer constituents in a large account
- Not contacting them often enough.

An everyday story of neglect in an experience

A B2B customer is installing a new computer system. The customer's project manager, an introverted person by nature, feels that he is not being consulted on important decisions. There have been a number of cases where his own team and the computer vendor have not included him in important emails or phone calls. At project meetings he feels he is being ignored, both by his own team and by the computer vendor who all tend to focus on his boss. The result of all of this is that he is feeling neglected.

What could be done to relieve the feeling of neglect in this customer?

The computer vendor should ensure that their teams understand different personality types and make allowances for them. Just because this person is quiet doesn't mean that he doesn't have feelings and is not important. The vendor should identify the key people in the project and make sure that they are involved equally in the loop. The vendor should build a good working relationship with this project manager and offer to mentor him in how to impose himself more on the project, if he wished.

Unsatisfied

Definition: Not being satisfied with the outcome; not meeting expectations; feeling worried and uneasy; feeling a lack of contentment or satisfaction.

If you are unsatisfied, you have not even reached satisfied, bearing in mind satisfied means "you got what you expected." We already know that even satisfied customers defect, so unsatisfied customers definitely do! If the customer is unsatisfied, it normally means they are disgruntled in some way or displeased with some aspect of the service. There may be a number of "feeder" emotions that could be identified before the end result of an overall feeling of being unsatisfied.

The typical causes of feeling unsatisfied are when:

- You don't understand or satisfy the customer's physical and emotional expectations
- Customer's physical and emotional expectations are not managed
- Items are not delivered on time
- Suppliers are unreliable
- Suppliers do not want to take responsibility
- Employees are not trained on customer expectation.

An everyday unsatisfactory experience

A young family had been looking forward to their holiday since booking it a number of months ago. They had looked at the brochure constantly and were particularly impressed by the size of the rooms, swimming pool and the amenities at the resort. Unfortunately, as they were traveling out of season, the weather was inclement on arrival. In addition, the bedroom and swimming pool were nowhere near the size they appeared to be in the brochure photograph. To top this, there were repairs being undertaken in the hotel as it was out of season and not all the amenities were available. On checking the small print of the brochure, it does indicate that some of the amenities may not be available. All this means that the family were unsatisfied.

What could be done to relieve the unsatisfied client?

The vacation company should understand that people look forward to their vacation all year and expect photographs of the swimming pool and bedrooms to be realistic. The vacation company should also inform all guests of any building work and of any amenities that are not available, even if it is in their small print. Customers should also be informed of the likely weather and be provided with entertainment when it is not favorable. Finally, they should provide an independent assessment by previous customers of the resort.

Frustrated

Definition: To prevent someone from accomplishing a purpose or fulfilling a desire; thwarting an attempt to achieve a goal; feeling you are wasting your time; feeling the process is inefficient; being inefficient.

If you are feeling frustrated, what you are trying to achieve is being thwarted in some way. Frustration can start by feeling irritated, annoyed or disenchanted and then lead onto feelings of being *disappointed*, *unsatisfied* or *unhappy*.

For example, we were working with a credit card company in the USA. The Emotional Signature measurement had shown that the "frustration" score was nearly double that of other companies in the financial services sector. After further investigation we discovered that customers were feeling frustrated for a number of reasons. The voice menu system was seven layers deep and frequently sent people to the wrong location. In addition, the website navigation was cumbersome and slow. Having established the root causes, we were able to focus on improving these and managed to get the company back to industry standards.

The typical causes of customer frustration are:

- Slow systems
- Bureaucratic procedures
- Long lines
- Inefficient processes
- Sending customers to different departments with no one taking responsibility
- Keeping customers waiting
- Making something that is simple, complex
- Putting customers through a process that is for the benefit of the company
- Asking customers to fill out numerous complicated forms, particularly when you already have the information.

Chuck Kavitsky, CEO Fireman's Fund Insurance Company, tells us how simple it is to frustrate customers:

> One of the horrors is to just read your own letters, which you've sent to your customers. Customers can get four or five different letters concerning an accident that could have been made into one. The letters are technical and not customer friendly. We know this has caused frustration with our customers so we have now changed these letters, to show the customers we value them. Again it's really getting into the nitty gritty of the process.

It is only by everyone in the business constantly testing your own Customer Experience that you can see what it is like.

An everyday frustrating experience

A customer has been looking forward to acquiring a satellite navigation system for his car. He is going on a trip to many different locations around the country in a few days and particularly wants it for this journey, as it would save a lot of time, stress and effort. The customer buys the device from a reputable national electronics retailer. On taking it home and installing it, he discovers it does not work. He immediately tries to find the phone number of the store on the website but it quickly becomes apparent that the company does not encourage calls as they have buried the contact details deep in the website. He's now starting to feel frustrated. Eventually the customer finds the HQ number and calls them. After some explanation he is informed the only thing that can be done is to take the unit back to the store. As his trip starts the following day, he has no choice but to stop what he is doing at work and take it back straightaway. On entering the store, he explains the problem. The product is checked as if he has done something to damage it. After some 25 minutes, he is finally given a replacement. At home that evening he tries to install the unit again. The same problem occurs. He is now very frustrated. It is too late to get a replacement for his journey. During his travels, every time he reads a map or gets lost, he is reminded of this experience and feels frustrated and annoyed. On returning home, he again takes the unit back to the store and is informed by a different assistant, in a "matter of fact way," that this type of satellite navigation system does not work if your car has an electric front heated windscreen. This was clearly the problem with the first unit as well. No thought is given to the time and frustration this customer has gone through.

What could have been done to avoid or relieve this frustration?

The frontline teams should be educated on the limitations of this unit. When selling a device, the customer should be asked if they have an electric front heater on their windscreen. The customer should be informed that the system is unlikely to work if this is the case. If this one simple question had been asked when the customer bought the first product, then none of this would have occurred. Clearly, this has also cost the company money dealing with the returns and potential loss of future business from this customer.

Disappointed

Definition: To fail to satisfy the hope or desire of a customer; not living up to someone's expectations; letting a customer down.

If someone is disappointed, it has gone beyond being unsatisfied. It means they had an expectation which has not been fulfilled. This can be the state before feeling depressed.

Dann Allen, vice president of business development in our Atlanta office, recently had a poor customer experience with a major hotel chain. He was attending a conference and on the last day, he wanted to check out late. The hotel front desk approved his late check-out – he was pleased and felt valued. However, the experience he was about to receive with the maid, bell captain and front desk staff destroyed these positive emotions. I'll let Dann tell the story:

I was beyond my time to check out late by about 15 minutes. The maid knocked on the door and so I let her in. As I had been an exhibitor at this conference, I had a number of boxes of trash to be thrown away. The maid called for the bell captain to help dispose of the boxes. Initially I was impressed with her friendliness and promptness to sort out my trash. I thought, this hotel is pretty good – friendly, courteous and understanding staff.

The bell captain came and I showed him which boxes should go and which ones I was taking with me. I felt I needed to watch him load the boxes but I couldn't as I had other things to do so I left him as it was quite a simple request.

A few minutes after he left, I checked the boxes and saw that one that I needed had been taken. I began to panic as the box had important documents that I needed. I rushed to the hallway to try to stop him but he had gone! I asked the maid where he would go and she said she was not sure. I asked if she could help me, but she said there wasn't much she could do other than to phone the front desk.

I called the front desk but realized I didn't know the bell captain's name. The maid didn't know it either! The front desk then told me I would need to come down and fill out a form so if my box was found they would know it was mine and I could claim it. They weren't going to attempt to find it, just get me to complete a form! Meanwhile my documents were on the way to the dumpster with some unknown employee. More by luck than judgment the documents were found and they asked me to complete a lost and stolen form. Clearly very bureaucratic. During this experience I felt a number of emotions, including frustration, irritation, neglect but overall I felt very disappointed with their "couldn't care less" attitude.

The typical causes of disappointment are:

- Not achieving the desires of the customer
- Not living up to the brand promise
- Service declining over a period of time
- Overpromising and underdelivering
- Taking the customer for a ride
- Being dishonest
- Saying one thing and doing another.

Unhappy

Definition: Not happy or joyful; sad or sorrowful: not satisfied; displeased or discontented.

If you are unhappy, you feel sad or sorrowful and this is a deeper emotion than just feeling unsatisfied. This can also potentially lead to a mood. This makes you discontented and you want to move on.

An everyday unhappy experience

Lorraine, my wife, was feeling very pleased with herself as after many years of encouragement she had done a considerable amount of the Christmas shopping online. She felt confident as this particular popular, online retailer had promised that all orders received at least five days before Christmas would be delivered before Christmas Eve. However, due to high demand and an underestimation of the resources required, they failed to achieve this, causing a huge number of emails and phone calls from customers complaining. Lorraine was one of them. Feeling very unhappy and stressed, Lorraine was forced to go shopping on Christmas Eve to buy the undelivered goods, which also cost more than the online prices. As if this was not enough, Lorraine then had to repackage the goods that were received some time after Christmas with an explanatory note and take them to the post office. She then had to spend further time checking that the credit had gone through on our credit card statement. Obviously, Lorraine was a very unhappy customer!

What could be done to achieve a better outcome?

The online retailer should ensure they have sufficient resources to deal with the enquiries and have a contingency plan they can call upon. They should be conservative with their delivery dates, as failure to deliver this year could affect purchases in further years. In addition, the retailer should have cancelled orders that were obviously not going to be delivered on time rather than leaving the order to be delivered late. Furthermore, they could have offered some compensation, additional refunds or vouchers as a goodwill gesture for the customer's wasted time and money.

The typical causes of unhappiness are:

- Not delivering things on time
- Something that is related to a proposed happy event as there is a higher level of importance placed on these occasions
- An event that culminates in the customer feeling sad
- The culmination of other negative emotions
- Being treated poorly by members of staff
- Being severely let down
- Being treated exceptionally badly.

Hurried

Definition: To cause someone to move or act with undue haste; to rush; the act or an instance of hurrying; hastened progress; haste; the need or wish to hurry; a condition of urgency.

If the customer is feeling hurried, this is typically because the organization wishes to process them as fast as possible. They are treated like a transaction on a production line and not listened to. They are feeling rushed, either by the organization or because of the things that are happening in their lives.

For example, a personal computer manufacturer we dealt with had established a process where customers would phone in and discuss their requirements. Using Emotional Signature we discovered that customers were feeling hurried. On investigation, it transpired that a number of customers were not very technically literate and therefore the agent had to explain the differences to them. One of the measures the agents were judged on was the length of the call. This caused the agents to "hurry" their customers so they could get their pitch in about price and hopefully close the deal, the main measure of success. We suggested they take away the time element and allow the agents to spend the required amount of time talking to the customers.

The typical causes of "hurried" in a Customer Experience are:

- The organization creates a process that is based on speed for their benefit
- Treating the customer as a transaction
- Not listening to the customer
- Not taking time to listen to the customer
- Measures that drive the wrong behavior.

An everyday example of being hurried

The customer has a new job and is relocating to a new town. They are under pressure to make this move and they are feeling hurried in a number of things, which is making them feel unhappy as there are big decisions to be made. Upon visiting the town, they are taken around a few houses by a realtor. The realtor is in a hurry to sell properties and therefore starts to put the customer under pressure to make a decision by saying that these properties will not be around for much longer and the prices will increase. This just adds to the feeling of being hurried and if it continues could lead to feeling stressed and unhappy.

What could be done to relieve hurried?

The realtor could realize how the customer is feeling and sympathize. They could calmly inform them of the speed that the market operates, therefore that the houses will sell quickly. The realtor should understand the customer's requirements fully and narrow down the search, thus saving time.

Irritated

Definition: To be a constant cause of annoyance; to be the cause of impatience or anger; when something "grates" on you.

If you are irritating a customer, it is something that can gall them or make them feel infuriated. There is a difference in what a customer expects and what is being delivered. Again, this emotion typically moves on to feeling disappointed, frustrated and unsatisfied.

For example, one of our B2B clients used to market their "below the line" services to blue-chip companies. On attending an exhibition and gathering prospective customer information, they proceeded to follow up on these contacts. They phoned them, emailed them and sent them hard copies of brochures. Our study showed they had managed to irritate the prospective customers who had been predisposed to use them. However, because of the incessant contact, these customers decided not to deal with them any further.

The typical causes of irritation are:

- Pestering the customer
- The customer not getting what they want
- Putting obstacles in a customer's path
- Sending unsolicited information
- Measures and reward schemes that drive constant contact
- Anything the customer doesn't like.

An irritating experience

On arrival, after a long journey, a tired couple entered the hotel and walked up to reception to check in. The receptionist was on the phone to another guest. After the call was finished, she said hello and then immediately the phone rang again. It was another guest asking for a shuttle service to the airport. When the receptionist finished this call, she apologized but informed the couple that she needed to arrange this quickly. After five minutes had passed, having radioed different people and arranged the transport, she finally turned to the tired, and now irritable, guests and started the check-in procedure. Guess what, the phone rang again and she answered it, adding a further wait for these guests.

What could have been done to relieve irritation?

This is another example of inside out behavior. No thought was given to the fact that guests would have traveled some distance and would be tired. Either the receptionist should not be taking the calls and someone else should be allocated this task or she should deal with the customers in a strict order. At the very least, they could have been invited to sit down and she would come to them. It always amazes us that customers on the phone are allowed to "push in" and get a faster or higher grade of service than the face-to-face customers.

We hope these examples give you an idea of the emotions we are referring to in the Destroying Cluster and some of the actions you can take to resolve these issues. In many cases, these emotions are being evoked simply because the organization is inside out or they are just not looking at things from the customer's perspective.

The following example is a case study from one of our clients we have been working with for some time. Hopefully this will bring to life the whole process, which will aid you in working out what you need to do in your organization.

Case study: IBM

IBM has earned the right to be one of the most respected brands in the world. In the past decade they have gone through a remarkable transformation. We have been pleased to be working with the customer-facing teams at IBM for some time in a division they call ibm.com. Contrary to their internal title, ibm.com is not just a web channel but also an extensive telephone channel selling and providing account management and support around the globe. There are some 6,000 employees spread all over the world dealing with their two main segments of business accounts, below 1,000 employees and large corporate accounts above 1,000 employees.

I first met Debra Cross, manager of client experience at ibm.com, some years ago at a conference I was speaking at in Florida. Having read our first book *Building Great Customer Experiences* she attended one of my workshops and we chatted afterwards. From my early days of dealing with Debra it was clear she had "got it." She was now on a quest to help ibm.com improve their client experience along with her team, in particular Tammy Luke Hughes. The good news was her vice president, Tom Dekle, was also very supportive and this is fundamental to a Client Experience program's success.

To set the scene, the ibm.com Superior Client Experience Team had embarked on a journey to improve their client experience in early 2004, they had established a virtual global team, set in place a strategy and already engaged in a number of internal studies, interviews, and client focus groups to determine where changes were required. They had established robust actions with some hundred plus individual actions being undertaken by people across the globe, all designed to improve their experience. I remember sitting at a meeting in Atlanta with Debra and Tammy and thinking to myself that they had undertaken this change in a very rigorous manner. We were impressed with the breadth and depth of this work.

It was clear they had addressed and were still addressing some fundamentals of the physical aspects of their client experience in areas like process, systems, people, and so on. Given the nature and stage of development as an organization this was the correct focus. While they had made significant progress they felt they weren't moving the dials enough. Therefore we were initially brought in to review their progress and suggest the next step they should take and help them recalibrate where they were going. After our work, one of our recommendations was to place more focus on the emotional side of the experience.

As an established client who has always been willing to innovate, they were keen to be one of the first worldwide organizations to discover their Emotional Signature. We are very grateful to them for allowing us to share the results in this book.

To set this in context, Figure 4.4 shows the Emotional Signature for business overall and the IT sector. Remember the higher the emotions that drive value, the better, so they are felt more. The lower the destroyer emotions, the better, so they are felt less.

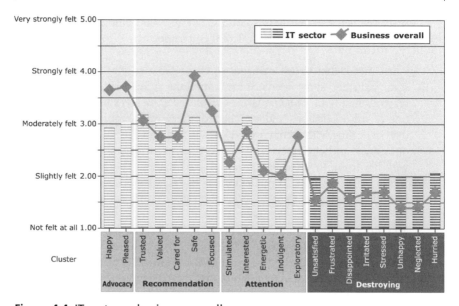

Figure 4.4 IT sector vs business overall

You will see from Figure 4.4 that the IT sector is behind business overall on the Advocacy Cluster and the Destroying Cluster. We believe this is because the IT industry has a number of unique challenges. For example, we have all wanted to kick the computer when it "hangs" or loses data for some reason. This generates a number of Destroying Cluster emotions. These and other reasons make this industry different.

When comparing the IT industry to entertainment (Figure 4.5), the IT industry is well behind on most of the clusters. Clearly, the entertainment industry, by its very nature, is trying to create happy customers. You will also see another extreme, banking, in Figure 4.5. Having undertaken a considerable amount of work in the financial services sector it is clear that this is a very "left brain" dominated area.

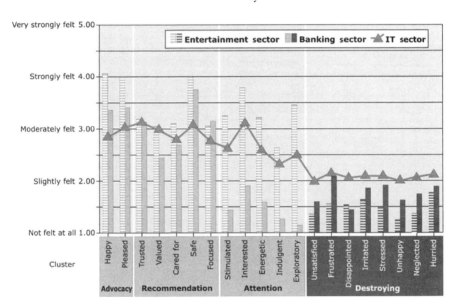

Figure 4.5 Sector comparison

In Figure 4.5, you will see that the banking sector's Emotional Signature is low, particularly in the Attention Cluster. I am sure you will agree that when you think of a bank you don't think of a place that is stimulating, interesting, indulgent, exploratory, and energetic!

In Figure 4.6, you will see the results from ibm.com. This illustrates that ibm.com are performing in line with the business overall in the Advocacy Cluster; ahead in most of the Recommendation Cluster; ahead on the Attention Cluster but behind on the Destroying Cluster of emotions.

You will recall from Figure 4.4 that the IT sector is behind business overall in the Destroying Cluster of emotions and, therefore ibm.com reflects the IT sector for this cluster (Figure 4.7).

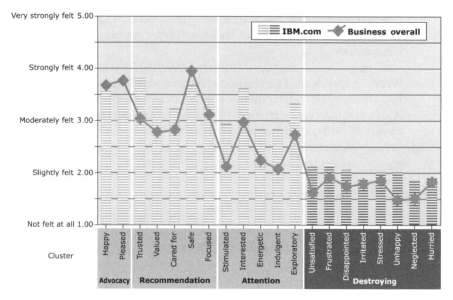

Figure 4.6 IBM vs business overall

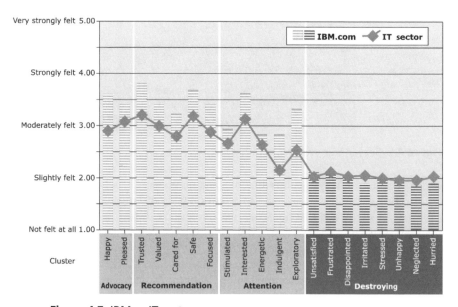

Figure 4.7 IBM vs IT sector

When going down from the cluster level to the individual emotions you will see that ibm.com are doing better than the remainder of the IT sector in the following emotions *stimulated*, *interested*, *exploratory* and *indulgent*. This is because they are challenging themselves to be seen as an innovative organization in the technology space. To a number of their clients, this technology is *interesting* and they are *stimulated* by these advances, wanting to *explore* the possibilities. Thus, these emotions bode well in this sector.

The other area that they are strong on is *trust*, after all this is "Big Blue" we are talking about. Consider that well-known business saying "You'll never get sacked for buying IBM." This is all about trust. It is no surprise then that their *trust* score is high.

Once we had conducted this analysis, we held a workshop with Debra, Tammy and a cross-section of representatives from IBM. At that workshop it was decided the primary focus should be on decreasing the destroying emotions as they were doing quite well in the other clusters. It was felt that if they could improve on these destroyers, then there could be some competitive advantage to be gained from the rest of the sector. As usual this means time and effort, therefore the executive team would need to fully understand the extent of this to support this new initiative. For the first time, using the Emotional Signature of Value we were able to calculate the effect this would have.

Emotional Signature of Value

In Table 4.2 you will see the financial analysis we created for them in their two market segments, over a thousand employees (>1,000) and under a thousand employees (<1,000). For obvious reasons we have put this in a percentage range and not the real figures. These numbers are illustrative but representative.

Table 4.2 Options of financial return of Emotional Signature

Improving Destroying Cluster	<1,000 employees % increase in revenue	>1,000 employees % increase in revenue	Total % revenue increase
To meet business overall	3–7	7–11	6–10
Improve by 1%	0.2–0.4	0.2–0.4	0.2–0.6
Improve by 5%	1–3	1–3	1–3
Improve by 10%	2–4	3–5	2–5

We looked at this financial projection from four scenarios: if we improved the Destroying Cluster to match the business overall and if we improved the Destroying Cluster of emotions by 1%, 5% and 10%, what would be the effect? You can see from Table 4.2 that each of these scenarios gave significant financial benefits and they can be different in different market segments. If we manage to simply reduce the destroying emotions to that of the business overall, they would generate an additional

6–10% of ibm.com's revenues
A significant sum of money

This does not include the additional cost savings that would be gained by doing this, from fewer complaints, fewer returns, fewer calls into their channels to fix problems, and lower customer churn rates.

Given the IBM margin, these figures would produce a substantial profit that would far outweigh any investment that would be needed to improve the Destroying Cluster of emotions.

On top of this you can add on the considerable savings that can be made by reducing the destroying emotions as far fewer customers will complain, they will not return so many goods, and so on.

Clearly the next step is to define what you would need to do to change this. We identified that the focus should be on elements such as:

- Improve the coordination of delivery – when selling a solution the parts can be delivered from all over the world and may not arrive on time. Sometimes a vital part is missing which can cause a delay in the implementation.
- Continue to improve the web navigation to the client's desired expectations.
- Improve the process of clients being transferred between departments.
- Ensure that all information is captured when the client calls to avoid asking for the same information twice.
- Reduce the time it takes to "activate" new clients.

There were a number more. Some of them reinforced existing standards while others were new and would require additional investments.

So a very impressive beginning for ibm.com, and the challenge will be to keep this change going. The work to improve the client experience at ibm.com continues today and our belief is that they are headed in the right direction.

We hope this gives you a good idea of the Destroying Cluster. Now let us move on to more positive emotions. Imagine that you want to gain customers' attention and attract them to your organization. How do you do that? What are the emotions that you should be evoking?

Note

1. From *Building Great Customer Experiences*. Organizations that are inside out look at what is good for them and impose that experience on customers. Organizations that are outside in look at what a customer wants and change their organization.

5 The Attention Cluster

"Oh look, there's a new restaurant opened up in town, shall we see what it is like?" said Lorraine (my wife). We have always been keen to explore new settings. We booked a table for that weekend. As we drove towards the restaurant we chatted about what it was going to be like.

On arrival there seemed to be a buzz about the place, everyone was very energetic and engaging. The manager was waiting at the door and greeted us, "Good evening Sir, Madam, welcome to our restaurant. It is so good of you to join us this evening. Would you like a table by the window or in the corner?"

"By the window please, the view is lovely over the river," I replied with a big smile. As we were seated, the manager said "We really hope you like the menu and have an enjoyable evening. John will be over to explain the menu and take your order, in the meantime can I get you a drink?"

Everyone was very engaging, smiling and attentive; the menu was very different, contemporary and interesting. The restaurant was something new, something different, and we were in exploratory mode. Lorraine and I had a very pleasant evening – so much so that on the way home we were discussing when we could go back. I realized I had been stimulated by the experience.

A few days later we went for a drink with a couple of friends. "We went to that new restaurant in town a couple of nights ago. It was really nice! The service was great and the food was even better! You should go," we said proudly as if we had discovered a new secret. "Yes, we have been thinking about going there as we have seen the ads in the paper and the flyers around town." "Why don't we go together in a couple of weeks," I suggested. "OK that's a date!"

Three weeks went by before we could get our calendars together. This time the waiters were not so attentive, not so energetic or engaging. The sparkle seemed to have gone. The manager was nowhere to be seen, the meal was nice, but that's about it. The reality was we were disappointed. We felt a little let down and a bit embarrassed that we had told our friends how great it was.

Another three months passed and again we decided to give it the benefit of the doubt. There was no longer a feeling of exploration as there had been before. Nothing had changed from our last visit with our friends. The feelings of energy and engagement of our first visit had totally disappeared, in fact I would go so far as to say it was now labored. It was now like any other restaurant. The menu hadn't changed; we were treated like a transaction. It is now like the other 15 OK restaurants within traveling distance of us. An opportunity lost to differentiate themselves.

This is a good example of the Attention Cluster of emotions at work (Figure 5.1).

In the beginning these emotions of *interested*, *indulgent*, *stimulated*, *exploratory* and *energetic* can give you a short-term lift. In this case this is exactly what happened. Their advertising and PR worked well, people knew about it. We were keen to visit and explore. On visiting the restaurant the experience evoked all the emotions in the Attention Cluster, so much so it made us tell other people.

The Attention Cluster is the *only* set of emotions that have a direct impact on short-term spend. However, that impact is short-lived if you do nothing to continue to stimulate these emotions. The effect of the Attention Cluster of emotions will wane if not continually reviewed and maintained. This cluster is a dangerous set of emotions as they can lull you into a false sense of security. We are sure that the restaurant management was very pleased with the initial influx of visitors, but then made the fatal error of letting complacency set in. Let us start by again mixing the feelings with the finances and look at the economic effect on this restaurant.

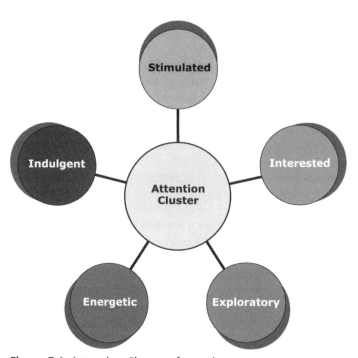

Figure 5.1 Attention Cluster of emotions

This restaurant had about 40 covers (individual table settings). At the beginning I would estimate that they had 75% occupancy over the week, taking into account lower numbers at the beginning of the week. This is evenings only.

■ The average bill was £40 ($72) per head

- Assuming 2 "sittings" in the evening gives us £2,400 ($4,320) per night
- 7 nights = £16,800 ($30,240)
- 52 weeks = £873,600 ($1,572,480) per annum.

Let's say this has reduced now to 40% of the covers. The same calculation means the turnover is £465,920 ($838,656) per annum, a reduction of £407,680 ($733,824) per annum! Quite a significant difference.

You could say that the Attention Cluster of emotions in this case are valued at £407,680 ($733,824), the difference between 75% and 40% covers. The environment, staff, menu, food quality, wine selection, and so on were all the same. The only thing that was different was the way that customers felt about it, the experience.

So just to be clear, the Attention Cluster of emotions has a *direct* link to spend. To put it very simply:

If you evoke these emotions in your customers they will spend more money with you

To that end, knowingly or unknowingly, these are emotions used by marketing to attract customers to their organization. Their advertising needs to be *interesting*, *stimulating* and *exploratory* so as to galvanize people into action, to attract customers to their organization, before they then move on to the Recommendation and Advocacy Clusters and become loyal customers.

The Attention Cluster is particularly effective in new areas and most people like new things, they are *interested* and *stimulated* by them, they like to *explore*. When everything becomes the same or monotonous, this is when they can slip into your subconscious mind and are not consciously acknowledged. This is very dangerous in a commoditized market. We have all heard people say things like "let's go somewhere new" when referring to a day trip or an evening out. Or you hear people saying "I don't want to go to the *same* place again." People crave something new, different and exciting. For instance I love gadgets – the exploration of them and playing with them is great. But after a while the novelty wears off and I quickly stop using them. It's fun to explore, it's fun to see something new.

Consider the cell (mobile) phone. Today they are fashion accessories for many people, particularly the young. The fact that the old phone still works is irrelevant. The new phone is more exciting, it has new features to *explore*. But the phone is also about fashion, and fashions change. This change can be a major asset in evoking the Attention Cluster of emotions. People love to explore the latest fashions and create new combinations of clothes. They love shopping and the *exploration* and *indulgence* of buying new clothes. Any organization that constantly refreshes itself like the fashion industry is helped by the Attention Cluster in its revenues.

You will see from Figure 5.2 that as we look into the DNA, given the same Customer Experience, over a period of time the Attention Cluster of emotions gradually declines from "strongly felt", to "not felt at all," if nothing is done to alter the experience. Therefore, the experience may start off well but these emotions will gradually decline if nothing is done to refresh the experience. There is a point, which will differ between organizations and customer groups, that we call "burnout." This is the point where the experience is no longer profitable, it has reached the point where trying to sustain it is not worthwhile.

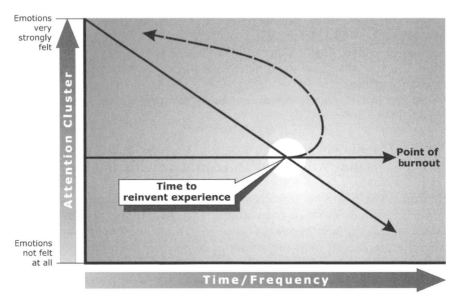

Figure 5.2 Emotional burnout

Let's get into the DNA in a bit more depth to establish what is happening here. "First impressions count" – we all remember the "firsts" of many things, our first kiss, first date and first job. Nowhere is this "first" more evident than in the Customer Experience. If a customer's first impression is good, they will come back, if not, invariably they won't. In your first experience you can feel the emotions to the maximum. The second time they are reduced as that excitement of the new experience has gone. You know what is going to happen, and while it may be enjoyable, it may not have the same intensity of emotion that you felt on the first occasion. You also start to see things in the experience that you didn't notice before as your brain was fully occupied on the first experience. You don't see that the walls have not been painted properly or the waiter's uniform is a little small. This can start to make you reappraise your first impressions. The second, third and fourth time you start to see the gaps. Have you ever noticed that when you are looking to buy a house, over the next few weeks when thinking back, your mind starts exaggerating the size of the house, and when you revisit it you are disappointed? The challenge, then, is to create an experience that gets the customer back for the second, third and fourth time and maintains the high standards of *stimulation*, *exploration*, and so on set by the first experience, or they will reach burnout. Now this is not always the case, but in our experience it is fairly typical. If you have created a very deep and detailed experience, then there are many aspects of it that you don't notice the first time which then keeps your experience optimized for the second and third time. For example, I like the Pirates of the Caribbean ride at Disney. There is so much detail that you see something new each time. However, if I rode this 100 times in succession it would become monotonous. Clearly, people do not do this and Disney knows this. Therefore the evoking of these emotions and the burnout point can depend on your products, service, and frequency. These are some of the things you need to consider when deciding on when your experience should be changed.

Take the fashion industry as an example. It is fortunate that the seasons change regularly as this provides a constant reason to change. Clothes shops like Zara, in Europe, use this knowledge to frequently change their range to attract customers. This is best described by Professor of Marketing Nirmalya Kumar of the London Business School who unlocks the secrets to the high street success of Zara:

> In 1975 Zara opened its first store in northwest Spain. By the end of 2005 there were 723 Zara stores in 56 countries. It has become Spain's best-known fashion brand with a winning formula based on its approach to the supply chain. Zara has been a pioneer in taking high fashion to the high street. With a team of 200 largely unknown designers, they create styles mimicking the latest on the catwalk, churning them out to the shop floor only weeks after their haute couture debuts. When Madonna toured Spain her outfit was copied by Zara designers. By the time she performed her last concert in the country, young fans were wearing the same outfit bought from Zara shops. Due to a frequent refreshing of stock, customers constantly return to stores to browse for new items. Most customers average 17 visits per year in comparison with only 3 visits to Zara's competitors.

Zara manages to evoke the Attention Cluster of emotions by constantly reinventing itself, resulting in a massive 17 visits per year. Therefore, keeping things fresh and new in a customer's mind will help evoke the Attention Cluster of emotions. Most organizations have a novelty value when they launch a new product or service. Does this new product, feature or service *interest* me as a customer; do I feel *stimulated* by its use and/or by the marketing campaign? Do I want to *explore* it, do I feel it is an *indulgence*, or do I feel *energized* by the product or the marketing campaign? Achieving this cluster of emotions is one thing, maintaining it another. Therefore, doesn't it make sense to measure these emotions to see where you are? Doesn't it make sense to do some research *before* you launch a product to discover how well your product or service and its marketing campaigns are likely to evoke the emotions in your customer, by customer group, by environmental setting? If you knew this then you could start to plan accordingly.

One of our clients was not measuring their customers' emotions, including the Attention Cluster. Like most organizations they would launch a new product, stimulate the market, but they only had the traditional ways of predicting how much and how long this product would be likely to remain in the market. In their market it was common to launch new products quite frequently so sometimes they would last 4 months, sometimes as long as 18 months. We have been asked not to mention the client, nor the industry as they now see this work as a competitive advantage.

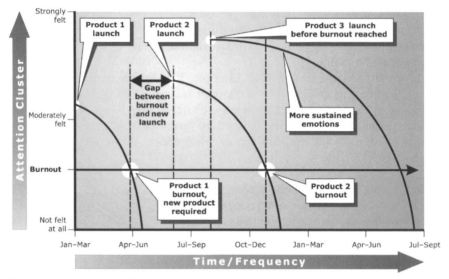

Figure 5.3 Attention Cluster and product launch

We discovered the following key insight into what was happening. This graph (Figure 5.3) is from our last presentation to them, having applied the Emotional Signature to their product launches. We discovered that the Attention Cluster of emotions was the most important to them. You will see that product 1, which was being launched as we began this study, did not enter the market with a very high emotional engagement and hardly stimulated the Attention Cluster of emotions at all, entering just over "moderately felt." Thus the product life cycle did not last very long and reached burnout much faster than they had hoped or planned for. Because of this short life cycle of product 1, product 2 was not ready for launch and thus there was a gap, causing a shortfall in revenues. The good news was we had some influence in product 2's launch and in a short time managed to advise on improving the product proposition and marketing strategy before it came to market. This improved the entry point of this product against the Attention Cluster and thus was more successful.

At the same time we were reviewing product 3 and for this we managed to undertake some research with customers on the product and the marketing approach to ascertain whether this would evoke more of the Attention Cluster emotions. Again, with some adjustments it did. The good news is they managed to launch this product before product 2 had reached burnout and thus gained enhanced revenue streams. We also increased the entry point on the Attention Cluster, so the emotions were more strongly felt from the beginning. Finally, and probably most significantly, we managed to embed some features into the product and the marketing campaign that extended the life of this product in the market. This company now uses this process with all its product launches.

Therefore we would recommend this to you when launching a new product to ensure the Attention Cluster of emotions is maximized:

1. Undertake pre-product launch research to determine the time/frequency/ exposure of your product or service.
2. Understand the emotional profile of your target audience, that is, younger customers like to change their cell phones frequently, older customers maybe not as often.
3. Understand the emotional effects of the Attention Cluster on your product and service.
4. Understand the emotional effects of the Attention Cluster for your marketing strategy and implementation.
5. With all this information predict the burnout point.
6. Plan new services to come on line at the time of burnout.
7. Measure and map the Emotional Signature throughout the product's life cycle.

The effect of this approach was dramatic for our client and has now been adopted throughout the organization. So, by taking this approach you will reveal more of the DNA of your experience and be able to predict future events more efficiently.

Some manufacturers use the "new" product or service tag to give them gains in these emotions for their advantage. Some, in our view, lack a bit of imagination though. You may recall a few years ago shavers for men had just one blade. They then launched two blades; at this point it was revolutionary! Two blades that give you a better shave. Next they launched three blades. And, you guessed it, next came four blades. I wonder what will happen next. Portraying things as new or the latest version appeals to the Attention Cluster of emotions, but, again, make sure that these claims are not too transparent otherwise it will have the reverse effect.

So how do you get customers to spend more? Simple, think of ways that you can evoke the Attention Cluster of emotions in your customers. This will increase customer spend. If you want to move your customers on to a medium- and long-term basis, then we would suggest you look at the Recommendation and Advocacy Clusters of emotions that we discuss in the next two chapters.

For now, let us look into the detail of the Attention Cluster and take each emotion one by one and give you a view as to what they are and how you can evoke these emotions.

Stimulated

Definition: To make a person excited and interested about your experience; making a person pay attention; an action that causes the body and mind to be engaged or become more active or enthusiastic.

If you are feeling stimulated, your senses are heightened, you are more engaged with what is happening in your experience, you are absorbed and your mind does not wander. You can feel enthused and inspired, which can lead to being motivated; motivated enough to buy something.

An unusual example of this is a company called Geek Cruises whose website (www.geekcruises.com) suggests:

> Take your mind on a vacation! Geek Cruises are everything you are looking for from a conference: stimulating seminars by the top names in the field as well as relaxation, adventure, and family time.

Here is one of the comments from a customer which sums up the experience:

> Thank you for a pretty great conference experience … I had a great time and learned a great deal. I'll definitely be recommending future Geek Cruises to my friends, co-workers and of course my boss! I think the best aspect of the whole thing was the total immersion factor as well as unparalleled after-hours access to the speakers. I have no negative comments except that it was too much fun, making coming back to work pure hell!

Typical actions you can take to evoke "stimulated" in a Customer Experience are:

- Introduce something new
- Create something imaginative that will take the customer by surprise
- Combine some learning and fun
- Think of a way to personally engage with your customer
- Get the customer to take part in some activity they enjoy
- Ask the customer stimulating questions
- Create a puzzle
- Do something different from what is expected
- Actively involve the customer in some way.

An example of a not very stimulating experience

A customer who is undertaking some repairs on their house visits a DIY home improvement store and buys a new electric sander. There are a number of tools on display and he is not certain which one is best for the job. The young store assistant is of no help so the customer buys the one that he thinks is best.

How this experience could become stimulating

Through their loyalty scheme, the store has asked customers some simple questions about their level of knowledge on DIY. The website offers "DIY tips" in video format, which are also shown around the store, enabling customers to see how they can undertake their task and get the most from their new tool. On entering the store, a woodwork expert is running a workshop on how to use the electric sanders. The customer knew to attend on this day as the company had emailed him with this information.

Interested

Definition: To gain someone's interest in something; wanting to give your attention to something and discover more about it; wanting to be involved with and find out more: someone or something that is unusual, exciting or has lots of ideas.

If your Customer Experience is interesting, you're clearly well on your way to engaging your customers. They will want to see more, you have their interest.

One organization that provides a great Customer Experience is Hamleys, whose tag line is "the finest toy shop in the world." We often take our clients on "safari" to Hamleys. A safari is an event where we take people around different stores to see good and bad experiences. Hamleys have a number of demonstrators throughout the store who are very interesting and engaging. They do not try the hard sell but, instead, entertain the customers and make them laugh to gain their attention. They undertake intriguing magic tricks that are unusual and exciting, making the experience very memorable. This investment pays dividends with increased sales.

Typical actions you can take to evoke "interested" in a Customer Experience are:

- Employ people with an interesting personality
- Understand the profile of your target audience and define what your customer would find interesting
- Change your experience periodically
- Design something unusual into your experience
- Consider different ways of getting your message across
- Consider showing some of the inner workings of your experience that people will find interesting to see how things happen. There are many successful "back lot" or factory tours that demonstrate to customers how things work.

A not very interesting Customer Experience

A customer is buying a new car from a dealer. He selects the model he wants and then a few weeks later collects the car from the dealer.

An interesting Customer Experience

Some friends of ours, Dave and Bernadette in the UK, recently bought a new Mercedes. Dave was given the choice of either picking the car up from the dealer or from the factory in Germany, which would include a tour. He chose the latter. They were then flown first class to Stuttgart to stay in a really nice hotel. All of this was complimentary for Dave, with a small charge for Bernadette. The next morning they were collected from their hotel, given a guided tour of the factory, with lunch, and then the car was wheeled out, sparkling and new, for a demonstration. They then drove their new car back through Germany and France, enabling them to stop overnight at a lovely chateau. Dave said the whole trip was excellent and made collecting the car a wonderful experience, adding "I'm almost tempted to get another Merc just to do the trip again!"

Such is the power of an interesting Customer Experience.

Exploratory

Definition: The feeling of wanting to explore; to enjoy the search; to discover more about something.

It is great to explore. Think about a time when you decided to go on vacation to a new country, you didn't know what to expect and you spent time exploring all aspects of the culture, the food, and the way of life. Exploratory is about being inquisitive. Have you ever stood and watched how people pick up food or other products and examine them? Being inquisitive can be one of the reasons we like mysteries and detective programs on TV. Exploring things can lead us on to problem solving, which again is a stimulator. "Why are they doing this?" "How does this work?" "What happens if I press this button?" These are all phrases to do with exploring.

This was taken from the thisisthelife.com website under "Expand your Horizons":

> Visiting the Pyramids, learning to make sushi or reflecting on Omaha Beach – read about some of the world's best cultural experiences and let us know your thoughts.
> Other popular destinations to explore:
>
> 1. New York Marathon, New York
> 2. Angkor Wat, Cambodia
> 3. Temples of Kyoto, Kyoto

4. The Great Wall of China
5. The Pyramids
6. Taj Mahal
7. Culloden Moor, Scotland
8. Pompeii, Pompei
9. Machu Picchu
10. Colosseum, Rome

An example of an exploratory Customer Experience

We were working for a large multinational in the US who are pioneers in telecommunications. They wanted to expand the use of their research facilities as a customer hospitality area. Customers are very excited about exploring the future and how the world of communications will affect them. We suggested the use of a futurologist for important events. They would give customers a problem that they may encounter in the future and let them explore how the new technology would help them.

Typical actions you can take to evoke "exploratory" in a Customer Experience are:

- Show the inner workings of something
- Let the customers discover by working things out for themselves
- Make your experience a bit of a puzzle, if appropriate, and add to the experience
- Change your experience regularly
- Make your experience interesting
- Create stages for your experience
- Understand your customer profile and how they would like to explore.

Energetic

Definition: The power and ability to be physically and mentally active; having or involving a lot of energy: to make someone feel energetic or eager.

If you feel energetic in a Customer Experience, you have gone beyond being engaged, you feel a sense of energy, stimulation.

For example, a client who runs leadership training for blue-chip companies decided to make the experience more energetic by moving to an outward-bound format, giving the delegates tasks to undertake, rather than just sitting in a class-room dealing with the theory followed by a few business games. They decided to put some energy into the event by getting the delegates out into the real world, undertaking exercises in the field which were not only stimulating to the mind but also to the body. This created a buzz and the scores of the event improved substantially. Incidentally, this also helped them with the "exploratory" emotion.

Typical actions you can take to evoke "energetic" in a Customer Experience are:

- Lots of physical and mental activity designed into the experience
- A high tempo throughout the experience
- Make use of senses, for example play high tempo music
- Get the customer involved
- Employing people who are naturally energetic.

A not very energetic Customer Experience

A UK credit card company is signing people up for new applications in a shopping mall. Customers are approached by lethargic salesmen and asked if they would like a credit card, with no passion or energy in what they are saying.

What could be done to evoke energetic in a similar experience?

The UK credit card company runs a game in a shopping mall where people can win £250 ($450) if they take part in a physically active game of limbo under a bar. They have high tempo music playing and a commentary from a lively person calling people to the game and then judging the event, thus building excitement and energy in the crowd.

Indulgent

Definition: To allow yourself or another person to have something enjoyable, especially more than is good for you; to give someone something they know they shouldn't really have or is special; something expensive or luxurious.

If you are feeling indulgent, this means that you are spoiling yourself, perhaps with a "forbidden" food that you know you shouldn't eat. If you are indulging yourself, it is with something that you normally value over many other things, it is special, for example eating popcorn is not particularly indulgent whereas caviar or Belgian chocolates are, due to their cost. If someone indulges you, they know that you would really like this and see this as being special and pampered.

Below are some examples of how organizations are using the "indulgent" emotion to advertise their products or experience. The first is taken from the website exhilaration.co.uk which sells indulgent products and services:

> Treat someone to the ultimate indulgence – a deluxe makeover designed to make you look and feel like a superstar. Try a makeover and photo shoot, or how about a makeup lesson? This one's a must for the girls …

On the website Lovemark.com, Jason from the UK talks about an indulgent chocolate biscuit:

> Tim Tams are the quintessential chocolate biscuit. It is Australia's best kept secret and features high on the list of essentials for all Aussie experts and travelers. The humble Tim Tam is legendary. Followers are loyal beyond reason because it presents indulgence in a biscuit. If you are after pure indulgence, try a "Tim Tam Explosion". Simply bite off 2 opposite corners of the biscuit. Place one corner in your mouth. Dunk into a coffee or hot chocolate – and suck your beverage through the biscuit like a straw. Before the biscuit melts and disappears into your beverage, make the melted contents end up in your mouth. If you have never experienced a Tim Tam explosion, you've never lived. This is the reason why a Tim Tam is a true Lovemark, it's not a biscuit, it's an experience.

This is from Thisisthelife.com:

> By yourself or with others, everyone deserves a spot of relaxation and indulgence. From tucking into a gastronomic delight to chilling out at one of the world's best spas sit back and enjoy the best the world has to offer.
>
> Most popular:
>
> 1. Pearl Resort on Taha'a Island, French Polynesia
> 2. The Jules Verne Restaurant in the Eiffel Tower, Paris
> 3. Espresso in Piazza Navona, Rome
> 4. Q Bar, Bangkok
> 5. Gran Bar Danzon, Buenos Aires
> 6. Belgian Chocolate
> 7. Bed Supperclub, Bangkok
> 8. Pacha Ibiza, Ibiza
> 9. Hand-made suits in Hong Kong
> 10. Sunsets

This is a personal example of indulgence:

> A number of years ago when I was still working for a blue-chip company, I was hosting a Sales Rewards program for the company's top sales people. We took them to the Palace Hotel in Sun City, South Africa. It is an enormous hotel and everything you could possibly want was offered. The restaurants were superb and they even took us on safari in the National Park which backs onto the hotel, along with a visit to a lion park, and then we traveled down to Cape Town and had a great time there. We made sure the sales team had a holiday of a lifetime and indulged their every whim.

Typical actions you can take to evoke "indulgent" in a Customer Experience are:

- Find out what your customers would consider indulgent and decide how to provide it to them

- Give customers something they would value and would not normally consider to be part of your service such as massages on flights.
- Be selective over who you provide it to, being indulgent also signifies this is not for everyone
- Consider some form of luxury – caviar, Belgian chocolates, butler service
- Look at other five-star companies who provide indulgent experiences and copy them!
- Pamper your customers.

A not very indulgent Customer Experience

The customer is attending a presentation the following day and is meeting the account manager for a meal the evening before as they are both staying in a hotel. The account manager takes the customer for a meal in the hotel and then for a few drinks. The following day they attend the presentation, have a few sandwiches at lunch time before booking a taxi for the customer to go back to the airport.

How to change this into an indulgent experience

A chauffeur greets the customer at the airport and takes them to a five-star hotel that the company has paid for. The customer is greeted by the account manager at the hotel reception along with one of his senior directors. As they know the customer is interested in football, they have arranged for the car to take them to a game that evening; the seats at the ground are great and a pre-match dinner is included. The next day the customer is picked up by the account manager and taken to the presentation, followed by a two-course lunch, perhaps including lobster, with the CEO. Finally, the account manager drives the customer back to the airport in plenty of time.

We hope this gives you a good idea of what these emotions are. Now let's try to pull this altogether and explain the power of looking at the Attention Cluster of emotions with a case study and relate it to the financial advantage of undertaking this type of work. As before, the details have been changed to protect the identity of our client.

Case study: HSR (high street retailer)

HSR is a large, internationally renowned retailer serving the youth market. HSR's brand is considered cool and particularly attractive to people with relatively large disposable incomes. They are generally known for their stylish clothing. HSR face a variety of challenges in their effort to be the retailer of choice for the youth segment. The cost of maintaining the attraction of their market segments has continued to increase with store upgrades and increased style cycle times. In addition, the youth segment in particular has become inundated with "me too" retailers and their associated marketing campaigns, so much so that the customer is spoiled for choice. HSR are looking to maintain their stellar brand image and market position but need to increase market share and revenues, and contain costs. As a key plank of their strategy, they recognize the need to deliver an experience that lives up to their customers' expectations but manage costs in areas that do not lead to increased loyalty.

Robert, the senior vice president of store operations, and Mary, marketing vice president, both recognize that HSR needs to continue to improve their experience and reduce their costs as a key part of their strategy. They have a concern over one of their key competitors "Kool Klothes," known as "KK," who are improving their market share – a worrying trend. They cannot understand why this is the case as their customer "satisfaction" measures tell them that they are better than KK.

We were asked to conduct an Emotional Signature of Value to understand how they were performing against KK from an emotional perspective. We were asked to identify how they could improve their experience. We were also asked what they could do to further enhance their "cool" image. So we conducted an Emotional Signature for HSR and KK stores and then compared the two.

Before we elaborate on this, let's set this in a bit of context. In Figure 5.4 you will first see the Emotional Signature of HSR against the retail sector. You will note that overall they are not doing too badly but when you consider this is targeted at youths with high disposable incomes, we would have expected it to be better than this, particularly on the destroying emotions of disappointed and neglect.

You can see from the Emotional Signature combining both companies (Figure 5.5) that KK are ahead on a number of emotions, and if not ahead they are equal to HSR. Not a good sign. KK are specifically ahead in the Attention Cluster and their innovative "Customer gets Customer" scheme is clearly working and paying dividends and at the same time reducing their marketing costs.

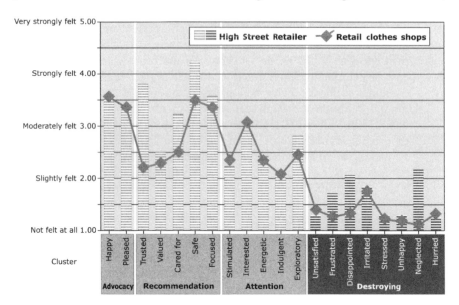

Figure 5.4 HSR vs retail sector

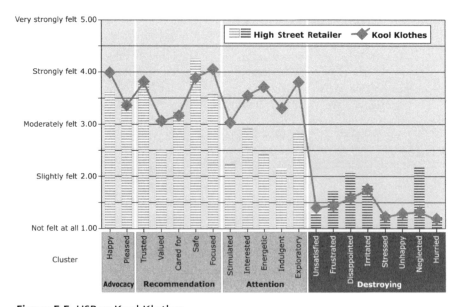

Figure 5.5 HSR vs Kool Klothes

The irony is that HSR's competitive Customer Satisfaction Survey completed on a monthly basis shows HSR to be ahead of KK, whereas the Emotional Signature shows that they are significantly behind, which would account for HSR's slip in market share.

NOTE: Since implementing the Emotional Signature in a number of companies we find this more and more, as typically organizations measure only 50% of the Customer Experience, the physical part, and do not address the other 50%, the emotional side, at all.

HSR's survey was only measuring opening times, lines, prices, range, and so on. Our belief was that they were measuring the wrong things. Granted they may be ahead in these areas but both companies were getting very high scores and to make a shift in this area is difficult. In addition, our challenge was, what did the customers think was important? These measures were years old and needed confirmation that they were still appropriate. For instance, what was important to them from an emotional perspective? They did not know. We find this common among many of our other clients. Only looking at the physical aspects of the experience can lull them into a false sense of security.

We decided to undertake a "competitive mirror" for HSR. This is an activity where we act as a customer and evaluate the Customer Experience of both HSR and KK with our trained eye, looking for clues as to why there were such significant differences between the two organizations.

This mirror revealed a number of key differences that accounted for KK's better scores. KK's employees were far more upbeat and energetic in their approach to service. The employees were also far more engaged than at HSR. At HSR there was that awful "Have a nice day" culture. In other words, we have been told to say "Have a nice day" but we really don't mean it! At KK the staff had more bounce, more energy and more commitment. It was clear that the store focused a great deal on culture. So much so that a number of employees from HSR had moved to KK. HSR found it difficult to retain the best people as KK and other stores were offering top wages and benefits as well. This was causing an employee turnover problem in stores. In addition, we discovered there was no training on how to emotionally engage with the customers and this was left to individuals' best endeavors. This became apparent in the different customer engagements we had with both sets of employees. KK were far superior.

We interviewed a person who had left HSR for KK and they confirmed that the leadership style of some of the HSR store managers was very macho and directive as opposed to the supportive and encouraging culture at KK. We also discovered in the mirror that, significantly, KK had introduced a personal dresser, which created the feeling of a very *indulgent* experience. This is something that was not available in HSR. The teenage girls thought this was great as the person was "cool" and had a terrific sense of style.

We found HSR was a far more "staid" store by contrast. In KK stores there were continuous in-store competitions, with customers being encouraged to take part. As customer's expectations were higher, due to the market position and pricing of the store, HSR were not living up to expectations. KK's loyalty card scheme offered some good discounts and promotions. The data collected from this was then used to offer discounts and a prize draw each week, with the winner being given two backstage passes to a pop concert. All this significantly drove KK customers to feel more valued than their HSR counterparts.

Armed with all our data and subsequent analysis, we presented our findings to Robert and Mary. We recommended the following actions:

1. Start to recruit store assistants with a high degree of emotional intelligence.
2. Implement a new training program and train people how to emotionally engage with customers.
3. Increase employees' pay and benefits to match the competition – this would be funded by the resultant decrease in employee turnover.
4. Put in place a personal shopper.
5. Offer a VIP ticket draw to key concerts for high value customers.
6. Create a method of differentiating the high value customers by making appointments and then ensuring that the personal shopper or the manager was available to take people around the store.
7. Measure all the Emotional Signature emotions monthly and set targets.
8. Implement an incentive program to kick-start the process.
9. Redesign the key processes to increase the occurrences of the targeted emotions.
10. Implement a store management training program on leadership skills.
11. Create a new recruitment process for managers.

12. Enhance the store refurbishment program to ensure the relevant emotions were focused on.

These were all accepted. At a subsequent workshop with Robert and Mary we then focused on which emotions we would increase and by how much. Having undertaken the costs on the above activity, we wanted to put the revenue streams together to get final board sign off. We had a great debate about the Attention Cluster and we gave them examples of new ways of marketing their stores and how their forthcoming store refit could be enhanced. During the workshop we decided to improve the score of the following emotions: happy, valued, disappointed, and neglect, as well as the entire Attention Cluster of: stimulated, indulgent, interested, energetic and exploratory.

Some of these were viewed as "outcome" emotions. For example, if they improved on valuing their customers, they would feel less neglected. If we improved the Attention Cluster and "valued" customers, they were likely to be happier. So for these emotions we played about with setting a target. After a review and a costed "project plan," it was decided that we should try to gain a 15% increase in these emotions. Putting this through our model, we could demonstrate that they would increase their sales by

£20,350,000 ($37m) per annum

Robert and Mary presented this to the board, receiving their full backing and the program was implemented. It is only when you start to link the feeling to the finance that you get true traction. The even better news is that to date they are on course to achieve their goals.

In summary, the Attention Cluster is significant in gaining new customers and enhancing the experience of existing customers. But once you have made the investment in gaining these customers, it would be criminal to ignore them. You should now aim to move them from "one-off" customers to customers who will recommend you. We can now move on to see how we can achieve this by using the Recommendation Cluster.

6   The Recommendation Cluster

I recently bought a new car. I knew exactly the car I wanted and there are three dealers within easy reach of my home. I began the task of visiting all the dealers to see what they had on offer. My first visit was to the dealer I bought my last car from. For those of you who read our last book you will know that they annoyed me during one of my car services and I wasn't really predisposed to giving them any further business. My visit to them just confirmed this. The second dealer was all over me. I hated it as she didn't leave me alone and I felt under pressure. With the third dealer, because of my last experience, I managed to stay out of the way of the salesman; it was a bit like playing hide and seek! I looked at the car I wanted, checked out the leg room, and so on, and decided that this was the one for me. The only decision now was what dealer and what price. This is where I passed the responsibility over to David Ive, our CFO. As the car was in short supply, none of the dealers would negotiate on price which created a very equal playing field, with price taken out of the equation. David was impressed with the dealer based in Milton Keynes, and his contact Peter. He decided to put a deposit down with them.

I still wanted to see the car to check a few details, color, accessories, and go for a drive, so I arranged to visit the dealer; however, they already knew the deal was done. Unfortunately, the only time I could make was a Saturday afternoon. When I arrived Peter was waiting for me and greeted me warmly. I noticed he wasn't dressed like the others and seemed to be in golfing attire. "Just come off the golf course?" I quipped. "Yes actually, today is my day off but I knew that you had decided to go ahead with us so I wanted to meet you in person and show you the car."

I was immediately impressed with his commitment and how much he clearly valued me as a customer. It would have been very easy for him to ask one of his colleagues to deal with me as he had already got the deal and we hadn't met before anyway. The chances are I won't buy another car for another two years, but for me he had already started the process of building a good relationship with that one action. We spent some two hours together. Peter took me for a test drive to put the car through its paces. As I got in to drive, I felt a little nervous as it reminded me of going out with my driving instructor, but he put me at my ease. When we got back he told me about the optional extras, including those that he considered a gimmick and not worth the money. Again I was impressed. This service continued all the way through to picking the car up, when again Peter was on hand to pass the car over to me. During the whole experience I felt that Peter was looking at me as a long-term customer, not just someone who would buy a car once and never be seen again. So far I have recommended this dealer to four other people, and that is in the short space of four months.

This is a great example of the Recommendation Cluster of emotions at work.

In the beginning we were looking at three different dealers which, as far as we were concerned, were all the same. At the end there is only one that I would recommend.

Let's look at some math. Let us assume the car was £15,000 ($27,000, cars are expensive in the UK) and a service twice a year at an average cost of £500 ($900) per annum, and I keep the car for two years.

Therefore over 10 years I may have five cars:
5 cars = £75,000 ($135,000)
Service = £5,000 ($9,000)
Total = £80,000 ($144,000)

Now let's assume I recommend eight people per year over that 10 years and assume 10% of them buy a car and have a service. Over 10 years, the additional revenue from my recommendation spaced out over that period will provide further sales of £477,500 ($859,500) on cars and service, plus my cars equals £557,000 ($1,003,500) – a lot of money!

Now imagine each of these people I recommend also recommends at the same rate. The math becomes mind boggling and could run into the millions. When you also consider how much less you would need to spend on the marketing budget to attract customers, the finances become compelling. All this from providing a good Customer Experience!

Was I treated like a £15,000 ($27,000) customer by the other dealers that would get the salesperson a commission, or was I treated like someone who could be worth £477,500 ($859,500)? Would you treat a customer who was worth £15,000 differently to one worth £477,500? I suggest that you would, and most organizations do by segmenting between consumers, small businesses and corporate customers. The greater the revenue, the more resources are allocated. Why then was I not seen by the other dealers as a £477,500 customer? What would they need to do to set me on this path? The answer is to evoke the Recommendation Cluster of emotions.

As you look at the Recommendation Cluster, you may consider them to be fairly fundamental or even basic emotions, but they are the foundations, the building blocks of customer loyalty. Without these, you do not have a loyal customer. Neville Richardson, CEO of Britannia Building Society, gives us his view of the emotions they are trying to evoke in their customers:

Our emotions are based around the "Recommendation Cluster of emotions". For us the key with our emotions is they build a long-term relationship with the customer. You clearly have to control the destroying emotions, that is, make sure your customers do not feel neglected, frustrated, hurried or irritated because then you're not actually "in control." The customers would say that when they are not stressed they feel "in control." If they feel out of control then this pressure will cause stress. So if I'm in control of my transaction, I don't feel hurried, this then becomes the foundation for a good experience.

Foundation is a good word. It is from this firm foundation that you can truly build loyal customers. We have developed what we call the "hierarchy of emotional value" (Figure 6.1), which is similar to Maslow's hierarchy of needs.

As Neville rightly indicates, in the beginning it is vital that you control the Destroying Cluster of emotions. These will never be eradicated completely but they need to be at an acceptable level so as not to taint your experience. It is then a matter of how you deal with the Destroying Cluster of emotions when they are evoked. Again, research will show you that you can gain loyal customers if you handle the service recovery in a professional and speedy manner. Once you have improved your Destroying Cluster, you then need to attract more customers. This is achieved by evoking the emotions in the Attention Cluster, that is, providing stimulating and interesting experiences as we learned in the last chapter.

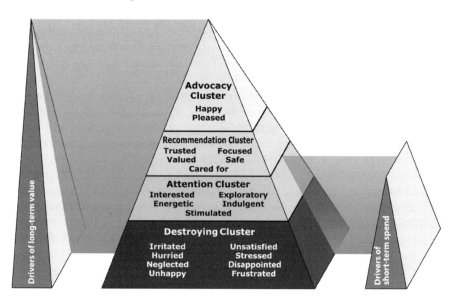

Figure 6.1 Hierarchy of emotional value

Once you have achieved this and attracted the customers, then you need to retain them and create loyal customers. This is broken down into two phases; the first phase being to evoke emotions in the Recommendation Cluster. The second phase is increasing customer loyalty and reaching the pinnacle to create "advocates" through the Advocacy Cluster. The significant difference between the last two clusters is that recommendation is *reactive*. For example, if a person asked who you would recommend, then you would inform them of an organization. Advocates are *proactive*, they will advocate the use of your organization without someone asking them. They may bring it up in conversation, for example, and just tell people about their great experience. As you will read in the next chapter, the Advocacy Cluster can be achieved through evoking the emotions of *happy* and *pleased*.

While these clusters are statistically independent, we believe that you will not reach the pinnacle of the "hierarchy of value" without passing through the Recommendation Cluster. For example you cannot feel *happy* when you do not feel *safe*. You cannot feel *happy* if you don't *trust* the organization you are dealing with. So, again, as in the previous two chapters, let us look in detail at these emotions.

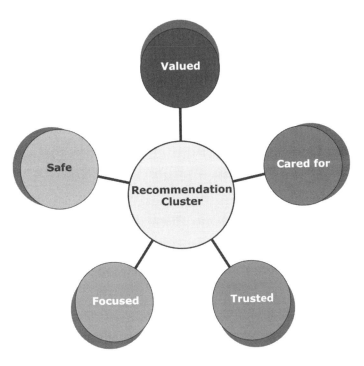

Figure 6.2 Recommendation Cluster

Safe

Definition: Not in danger or likely to be harmed; things which do not involve any risk; a state, or a place, where you are safe and not in danger or at risk; the feeling of security.

Safety is clearly a basic requirement in many experiences. There are the obvious cases of traveling in a car, plane or ferry where the need for safety is paramount, but customers also need to feel safe in their environment. Consider a hotel in a rough area; do the guests feel safe enough to go out at night? Does a manager holding a meeting in the hotel feel responsible for the safety of her people and choose to finish the meeting early. Safety is not just about bodily harm; it is also about the protection of things that are important to you, for example the safety of an important document, customer data, personal details, financial details, intellectual property rights, and so on.

The messages of safety are all around us – road signs, fire exits, warnings on food, tools, toys – the list is endless. These are all addressing the issue of safety. Here is a typical example taken off the MSN website on the safe use of the web:

> Ensuring that young people can experience the wealth of knowledge and communication opportunities on the internet safely is one of our top priorities. Here are some resources that will help:
>
> 1. How to stay safe online
> 2. How to keep your account secure
> 3. What to do if you have safety or security worries about MSN products
> 4. Report abuse and troublemakers on our services
> 5. Crack the code! Online awareness for teens
> 6. Virtual Global Taskforce – The Police Online
> 7. How does Microsoft work with the Police?
> 8. NEW: Read the MSN cyber-bullying report.

However, as we indicated, it is not just about physical safety. It can be the safety of anything that you value. Here is a further illustration from one of our IT clients:

> The IT company asked us to look at their experience selling systems to corporate accounts. It became clear that customers were concerned about the integrity of their system. This is not something the IT company ever concerned itself with. The reality was the system was very secure and they had, wrongly, made the assumption that customers would know this. Using Emotional Signature we discovered that "safety" had a very low score and therefore advised that all sales and marketing literature, as well as demonstrations, highlighted the safety features.

Typical actions you can take to evoke safety in a Customer Experience are:

- Consider your customer's safety in everything you do and explain to customers
- Use language that calls to mind safety, for example secure, protected, locked, sheltered, and so on
- Reiterate safety messages and place in prominent positions
- Provide case studies showing how the system has worked before
- Inform the customer why this is a sound decision
- Take them through a logical process and show why this is a logical and safe decision.

Not evoking a feeling of safety

A customer is checking into a hotel and is afraid of a potential fire after a previous, poor, experience. He asks the receptionist where the fire doors and assembly point are. The receptionist points to the fire doors and explains where the assembly point is and then checks the person in. Nothing more is said.

What could you do to evoke safety in this situation?

When the customer asks for the location of the fire doors and assembly point, the receptionist picks up on the fact that the customer is potentially not feeling safe and so asks if there is a problem. The customer explains he was involved in a hotel fire a few years ago. The receptionist listens with obvious concern. She tells the customer that she will book him into a room on the ground floor and next to a fire exit. She also arranges for the porter to take the customer's bags to his room and personally show him the escape route. When the customer is in his room, he receives a phone call from the manager asking if everything is OK and indicating that he knows that this customer had been in a hotel fire. He reassures him that the hotel has had a full test of their fire alarm system and the fire department had given them a clean bill of health.

Cared for

Definition: The feeling that someone cares for you; the process of protecting and looking after someone or something; continuous treatment in a caring manner; to feel protective and kind towards someone; to look after someone or something.

Caring is an important emotion. Again it can encapsulate a number of emotions. Think about when you feel cared for; you will probably trust that individual. If you feel cared for, it demonstrates that the person values you. If you care for someone, it shows that you think the person is important to you and worth looking after. It is very easy to give signals to customers that you don't care and a surprising number of customers receive these signals every day. Table 6.1 gives some examples.

Table 6.1 Combustion points

Not caring	Caring alternative
Putting customers on hold for long periods	Don't put them on hold for long periods! Define what is causing this delay, maybe lack of knowledge by agent, and so on, and fix it. Tell customer how long and why the call will be on hold. Increase staff numbers
Not listening to customer requests	Listen to customer's requests and repeat the information to confirm you have fully understood
Not passing them to another party without explaining what they want	Do a warm handover with an explanation of the situation/problem so that the customer does not have to repeat everything
Not considering their pre-experience	Consider the emotional state of the customer entering the experience, for example they will be annoyed because they have received an incorrect bill
Calling them at home in the evenings using predictive dialers resulting in silent calls	Don't! Or only do this with the customer's consent. These calls are all about being efficient for the organization and not about caring for the customer

These are some typical examples of what we call "combustion points" in a Customer Experience. They are normally embedded in the process because the organization has not thought through their experience design. Our firm belief is that your experience should be "deliberate." We typically find that most experiences are what we would call "consequential," that is, they are as a consequence of a number of factors. This is something we addressed in our last book *Revolutionize Your Customer Experience*. It is only by creating a deliberate Customer Experience that you will achieve consistency, which is vital for creating a great experience that makes financial sense. The emotions that drive value need to be designed into your experience as they have been at Build-A-Bear Workshop. Maxine Clark, CEO, explains how they have managed to do this, and demonstrate that they care for their customers by focusing on their needs:

We work at making it a consistent experience, but we also work at letting our Bear Builder™ associates use their own imagination and talk to each Guest as individuals to create a personalized experience. So if you asked "Are you making this bear for yourself today?" and they say "No it's for my grandma," "So, what are your grandma's hobbies?" "She loves the garden." "Well, we have the perfect outfit, does she have bunnies in her garden or do you think she'd like kitty?" We help guide them down the path, so that by the time they were done, they had created the most personalized gift possible for the person they're buying for. This makes the customer feel valued and stimulated and shows we care for them.

To show we are thinking of our Guests we ask if they have a budget: How much do they want to spend today? "Oh, that's no problem; we can help you with that." Some people say "I just want to buy a really soft, cuddly stuffed animal," and they walk out with a stuffed animal, with a bow around it, or ribbons on it, that's all free.

All a deliberate experience, all focused around the customer, all demonstrating "caring." The other way of providing a caring experience is to ensure that you recruit people who are naturally caring people. If you then create the right work environment, they will undertake random acts of kindness without being told to do this. A good example of a caring experience is from a friend of ours, Fenella Wallis, who works for the John Lewis Partnership (a large department store chain based in the UK):

> One day while working in the store during an unusually hot summer, Fenella received a phone call from an elderly lady, who ordered a flat-pack fan. (UK weather doesn't warrant air conditioning in homes). As John Lewis didn't deliver to the area she lived in, Fenella decided she would deliver the fan herself, on her way home that night. When she arrived, the lady was very pleased with Fenella's thoughtfulness. However, it quickly became apparent that the lady did not seem to know how to put the fan together. Fenella decided to assemble it for her but on reading the instructions realized she needed a screwdriver, which the lady didn't have. So Fenella drove to her house, collected some tools, and drove back to assemble the fan. Fenella didn't think anything of this and didn't mention it to anyone at work. A few days later she was approached by her manager who had a big smile on her face! The son of the lady had sent a letter to the general manager of the store thanking Fenella for her kindness. Fenella was then recognized by her management team and used as a good example for other employees as to how they should care for their customers.

A great story and an excellent example of a caring experience. Let's hear from Maxine Clark on what Build-A-Bear workshop does to recruit people who care.

> We hire people with this kind of passion and energy. The first thing we look for is people who care. You can train people how to work registers and how to do numbers, but you can't train people to care, that's what they come with from their background, from their work experience.

Typical actions you can take to evoke "cared for" in a Customer Experience are:

- Spend time listening to the customer
- Demonstrate empathy
- Employ people who are emotionally intelligent and naturally good at caring
- Create a caring culture
- Anticipate customers' needs
- Understand customers and show that you understand them
- Show customers that you are interested in what is best for them, not the organization
- Give people the space to be caring.

Trusted

Definition: to have belief or confidence in the honesty, integrity, goodness, skill or safety of a person, organization or thing; the belief they will not harm or deceive you; the belief that you can trust someone or something; keeping your promises.

Trust is a fundamental emotion. You need to be able to trust the people, and therefore the organization, before you do business with them. If you trust an organization, this will give you confidence. It is when you do not trust an organization that it can build in a massive cost to the business. For instance, if you do not trust that the engineer will come to fix your telephone line because they have failed to keep appointments in the past, typically you will contact the call centre "just to check" that the engineer is on their way. This takes up both the customer's and company's time and is borne out of a lack of trust. The example of breakfast at the restaurant in Chapter 5 is all about a lack of trust of the customer.

This is a common area in which we find organizations perform badly. All organizations want their customers to trust them but they do little to gain or repay that trust. For example, banks have pens on chains, some stores operate a poor returns policy, or you are told that goods will be delivered the next day and they aren't. When you call to ask where the delivery is, because notes have not been recorded about the previous call, the company effectively say you are not telling the truth about calling before. Commonly, in many organizations people say they will call you back and they don't. There are many, many examples of organizations not keeping their promises.

The classic area in which organizations demonstrate that they do not trust customers is in customer complaints. How many times have you complained about something and the person dealing with this has said "you need to put this in writing." Why? It's as if they don't believe you until you have written it down! If they were "caring," they would listen to your complaint or comments and write them down for you, if they need this internally for some reason. Typically people in the call center are not empowered to make decisions, so pass you over to another team. In essence, the company is saying we don't trust you as the customer, and it is also a management signal to employees that they don't trust them to make a decision either. The customer complaints team or manager then asks the customer for proof or says they will look into the matter and get back to you. Again, saying "we don't trust you so we need to look into this." However, all the statistics reveal that customers will settle for less compensation the quicker you can deal with their complaint. At Ritz Carlton they give all their employees up to £1,100 ($2,000) to sign off *any* customer complaint because they trust their people to make the right decision. Clearly, their employees do not give the full amount for all complaints and sometimes not at all, it is left to their judgment of the situation. Stena Lines, the ferry company between Scotland and Ireland, do the same with €1,000 (£670; $1,200).

This is from one of the world's major credit card companies that took part in our B2B research:

> More and more we are seeing that it is important to build trust with customers, making them feel valued is giving them the benefit of the doubt. We have listened to customers who feel that we are not on their side and don't have their best interests at heart. We now always try to be on our customer's side so if they call up and say they have a dispute and have received a charge they don't think is valid, our response is consistently to be superior to almost any other credit issuing institution.

Typical actions you can take to evoke "trusted" in an experience are:

- Do what you say you will do
- Give the customer the benefit of the doubt
- Do not base your experience on the 3% of people who are out to defraud you
- Do not treat all customers as criminals
- Empower your people on the front line to make decisions and sign off significant amounts of money for customer complaints
- Call customers back when you say you will
- Be transparent
- Involve customers in your organization.

A "not very trusted" Customer Experience

A removal company arranges to visit a customer's house to provide a quote on the cost of their move. The company representative does not arrive on time and doesn't phone. The following day the removal company phone and apologize for not attending and give a lame excuse. It all feels rather half-hearted. On the day of the house move, they arrive three hours late. During the move a valuable piece of china is chipped but the company doesn't tell the customer. When the customer notices later that day, the company deny it is their fault.

What you could do to evoke trusted

The removal company representative arrives on time to give the estimate of costs and fully inform the customer of the process. The van driver calls 30 minutes before arrival to confirm they will be there on time. They can do this as the company does not overbook and therefore knows the vans are available to move the customer on time. When they accidentally chip a piece of china, they immediately inform the customer and confirm this will be covered by their insurance. When they have finished the house move, the owner of the business calls the customer to ensure that everything has been completed OK and they are happy. The following day a bunch of flowers is delivered from the company wishing them well in their new home.

Focused

Definition: to give considerable attention to one particular person, subject or thing; the feeling of being "zeroed in on" or being "in the zone"; to be absorbed, engaged; to have a single focus.

On the face of it "focused" is quite an odd word until you peel back the onion and look at what it means. If you are focused you are totally absorbed by the experience, nothing else matters, you feel determined. The feeling of focused means all these things. It means you are concentrating on the experience and as such nothing else is disturbing you. This can be very enjoyable for many people. For example, people's hobbies evoke these emotions, they are absorbed and focused on the hobby. A children's charity we interviewed in the UK said this when talking about one of their suppliers:

> For the outsourced donation handling, I think "focused," "cared for" and "trusting" with our new supplier. I think we are "cared for" but also "valued" and I think that comes across in many ways, for instance if we want something done urgently or we don't agree with the time scales, they will change them.
>
> We did have a supplier who collected our donations. They were terrible. They made me feel stressed, they made my team stressed, they were uncaring and bureaucratic. They were not dependable and weren't flexible. All this was very shortsighted as overall they didn't do what they said they would do, they didn't deliver. We did not trust them. It was a contract that we decided to end because of their poor service and then we went looking elsewhere.

A not very focused experience

We were reviewing a Customer Experience for a B2B furniture supplier in Europe. We noticed that during an important presentation, the customers were very switched off as the supplier spoke about their range of chairs, tables and services. You could see people doodling during the presentation and emailing on their BlackBerry devices.

How to change this into a focused Customer Experience

We suggested that they needed to make their presentations more focused around what the customer wanted to see and to include a factory visit. Therefore, for the next session we ensured that the guests were asked beforehand what they wanted to cover. The presenters, who were more charismatic this time, started by talking about the workplace of the next 10 years and how the demographics will be changing along with the implications to business and the office environment. A tour of the factory followed. You could see the customers were more absorbed, as this time they were more involved, everything was carried out at a quicker pace to keep their interest, and the focus didn't wane.

Typical actions you can take to evoke "focused" in a Customer Experience are:

- Be clear what you want the customer to focus on
- Listen to the clues that tell you what the customer wants
- Do not offer too wide a range – less is more
- Use the senses to provide an engaging experience
- Provide the sensory environment where the customer can concentrate and not be distracted
- Keep the experience engaging by not allowing time for minds to wander
- Ensure that you do your homework on your customers so as to understand their requirements fully and then provide them.

Valued

Definition: To feel appreciated by an organization; to be acknowledged by their actions as being important. To be treated in a special way; to be held in high esteem and prized.

If your customer feels valued, this can be one of the most important emotions they feel as it sums up a number of actions. If they feel valued, it means you are not treating them like part of a process, instead you have acknowledged how important they are to you and that you value their business. All too often customers do not feel valued and are treated as transactions.

A recent study by IBM[1] shows that US consumers want banks to *value* their business, understand their financial goals and provide financial advice. This study reveals that 66% of customers *don't feel valued* by their bank and because of this they will not commit to deeper relationships with their bank. Furthermore, 74% of customers believe the bank's marketing offers are irrelevant and only 36% believe that employees are actually listening to their needs and will then act on them. This results in 50% of their customers claiming they would not consider them for new services.

The study goes on to indicate that customers consider that banks have made strides in their physical measures, getting this right 52% of the time, but fall short on the emotional aspects, only achieving what the customer wants 26% of the time. The emotional aspects that customers attribute importance to in gaining their advocacy include drivers such as valuing their business, understanding their goals and providing meaningful advice. This supports our thoughts on the subject and also relates to the Recommendation and Advocacy Clusters we talk about in this book.

For example, we were asked to review a financial services company's Customer Experience. We were quick to point to the practice that we really dislike of offering special offers to new customers and not existing customers. This client was offering better rates to new customers and when an existing customer phoned and asked for a similar rate, they were told they could not have this.

In one conversation we heard, the customer asked if they could close their account and reapply to get the deal. The customer was informed there would be a penalty charge if she did this. We said this sent out a very clear message to customers that what the organization values is new customers, not existing ones. Surprise, surprise, the Emotional Signature score of feeling valued for existing customers was low and the churn rate was above industry average. To make matters worse, the penalty clause also indicated that "once we have you we will lock you in and you can't escape!" The customer then feels disappointment and dissatisfaction, eventually leaving when financially viable. A change in both these policies soon turned the situation around.

Typical actions you can take to evoke "valued" in a Customer Experience are:

- Ensure your people treat all customers as valued customers
- Get the organization to look at the lifetime value of a customer
- Provide the customer with special discounts for length of time with the company
- Send customers a "birthday card" on the date they joined
- Celebrate faithful customers, acknowledge the time they have stayed with you – American Express has "Member since ... "
- Take time and listen to the client
- Thank them for their continued business.

A "not very valued" Customer Experience

The customer has been buying training services from a supplier for five years. This is a very transactional process where the customer places the order over the phone. The customer never feels they are valued by the supplier. They are approached by another training company and they are now considering moving. Ironically, because of this, the incumbent supplier has started to take more interest in them.

A valued Customer Experience

The customer has been buying training services from the company for the past five years. Each year on the anniversary of their first order, the customer receives a thank you card and a box of chocolates, as they do at Christmas and on their birthdays. In addition, the CEO of the company implements a detailed review of their performance every six months which the customer attends. The company also involves the customer in new product development to show they value the customer's input. A regular customer satisfaction survey takes place every three months and the results and action plan are shared with the customer. Finally, their account manager has been with the company for five years. They get on exceptionally well.

Hopefully, these examples give you an idea of the Recommendation Cluster of emotions. Just to reiterate, these are the emotions that give you the basic building blocks of customer loyalty – they are the foundation. As we mentioned before, these emotions need to be designed into your experience. You will recall from Chapter 3, Simon Fox, the MD of Comet, discussing how they have been developing a "deliberate" Customer Experience in their stores using Moment Mapping®. This design work has now spread to the home delivery service of the electrical appliances they sell. We'll let Simon pick up the story:

> Due to the outstanding success of the deliberate customer journey in stores, we are now repeating the whole exercise for our home delivery service. This has been even more successful than the stores! As a retailer we hadn't focused enough on the home delivery experience. But the reality is it is during this part of the journey that you are actually in the customer's home. It's much more personal than the customer visiting the store.
>
> We were a little concerned that the drivers would not see it as part of their role but we couldn't have been more wrong. Our drivers absolutely love this new approach and have embraced it. We have given them training on their deliberate journey and on how to approach customers, for instance the words they use when they call the customer before arriving. We also scripted little dramatic touches such as wiping down the product when they leave, or, if it's raining, rolling out the appropriate carpet protection. They also now wear footwear protection so as not to bring rain and mud into the home. We also now ask the customer how they would like us to deal with the packaging, making it clear that we do in fact recycle packaging as well as their old appliance, which they may not have been aware of. We also leave them with a little brochure with a clear phone number so if anything should go wrong they know who to call. Finally, and most importantly, we say thank you for shopping at Comet, a very deliberate touch at the end of the experience to show we value them and we are grateful for their custom. Customers really like these little touches!
>
> The results for the deliberate home delivery journey have been quite spectacular.

Let's now try and bring this all together by giving you a case study on a financial services organization that has undertaken the Emotional Signature.

Case study: FSP (a financial services provider)

FSP are a large US-based financial services provider with a strong and growing market position in the UK. Their growth is based on exploiting underserved portions of the market, and their hidden competitive advantage is their "savvy" financial analysts and actuaries. They hire young innovative thinkers who approach the market from a variety of angles. As a result, they have created a portfolio of products that are unlike any others on the market. Their competitors were slow to follow and, when they did, they found that their more traditional culture did not lead to the more radical thinking that was required to serve these highly profitable but slightly more risky markets. However, in recent years their competitors have strengthened their teams with more freethinkers and less risk-averse senior management, increasing their capacity in this area, and they are now taking customers away.

Unfortunately, due to their focus on unique products, FSP did not place much emphasis on their Customer Experience, particularly their post-acquisition experience. The competition is now starting to provide a real choice and a better experience. While customer satisfaction has remained stable over the past few years, for the first time FSP has started to see complaints increase as customer expectations have matured but their experience hasn't. What we discovered through the Emotional Signature is that as they have grown, their experience has got worse. Customers are no longer simply grateful that a reputable firm is providing a product they require, this is now a given and they want to be treated well. FSP wanted the Emotional Signature to assess why satisfied customers are complaining and leaving, even when they are satisfied with the products, which seemed to be a conflicting message for some in FSP as they are so product focused.

We were invited into the company by the newly appointed Customer Experience vice president, Gus. He had seen Qaalfa Dibeehi, our vice president of consulting and thought leadership, speak at a conference, and wanted to talk further. The issue he faced was that everyone had an opinion about how to improve the Customer Experience and there was a real appetite for change by his senior vice president but he was not certain where to start and how to deploy his resources. Our first step was to undertake Emotional Signature at different levels of the organization. They had two customer segments, low and high value customers. A high value customer was one that used more than three products from FSP. These customers used three channels: web, telephone and face to face (f2f). From our discovery work and conducting a Customer Mirror (a walk of the customer journey), we were able to show a cross-matrix of results from these segments and what we found was fascinating.

As you will see from Figure 6.3, the lower value customer segment has a more positive overall score than the high value, which seemed counterintuitive. Most organizations tend to look after their high value customers but FSP had grown over the past few years and this expansion had caused problems. We discovered that the more products and services you took from FSP, the worse your experience became. We also discovered that the higher value customers were feeling more of the Destroying Cluster of emotions, particularly frustrated, neglected and hurried, than the lower valued customers. Some of this was a reflection of the fact that these customers expected more as they had more products with FSP, but they weren't getting the service they deserved.

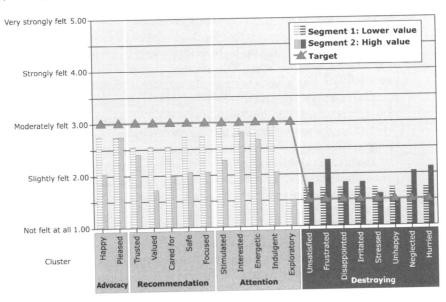

Figure 6.3 FSP: current vs target scores

FSP had, in the main, done a good job on the Attention Cluster, but again the lower value segment was better than the high value. On further examination, we found that this was because the lower value segment were quite excited by the niche products being offered and were typically new customers. Once you had been with FSP for some time, the novelty tended to wear off, as you can see from the Attention Cluster for high value customers who have a lower score. Of particular concern was the Recommendation Cluster. We discovered that their customer churn was very high. Effectively they were getting customers and then losing them, which was also costing a great deal in acquisition. One of the reasons was that it appeared FSP had very different experiences across their channels. In our Customer Mirror, we were surprised how they treated, or more to the point didn't treat, the high value customers in the telephony channel.

For example, when customers had more than one product, some of the cracks in the organization started to show as they were asked to deal with different parts of the organization that specialized in that area. If you spoke to an expert in one area, they did not really understand the offering in another area and thus you needed to be transferred. If you were a low value customer with only one product, you only had one expert to deal with and the world looked fine. However, as you then bought more products, you discovered that to get the best service you had to find your own way around the organization. This resulted in the high value customers feeling neglected and frustrated, as indicated in the Emotional Signature results. This then spilled over to the other clusters of emotions.

We further discovered that the high value customer didn't feel valued, as again the Emotional Signature confirmed, they were being treated like a product and were being passed from department to department. This was particularly true in the telephony channel but less so in the f2f channel. We discovered the FSP f2f employees tried to make up for the inadequacies in the company's organizational structure and were the glue that kept everything together, but at a price. For example, in the telephony channel, all too often people were passed from pillar to post with little introduction, the cause of some of the frustration and feelings of neglect by the high value customers. This, then, encouraged customers to contact the f2f channel far more than they needed to, as they knew they would get an answer. In some cases, they were being used as a type of switchboard, with customers asking "who do you think I should talk to about this." This showed their contact strategy was not clear to the customers and the irony was this was forcing them to deal with the most costly channel, f2f. We therefore suggested to Gus that his first priority needed to be the high value customers in the telephony channel.

What we encountered were some classic mistakes made by an organization that is inwardly focused rather than focused on the customer. After our analysis, we presented our findings to Gus and his team, and made the following recommendations:

1. Undertake further research to find out why the customers were calling the f2f channel and rectify the underlying issues.
2. Set in place a clear contact strategy for the customer.
3. Inform and train all employees on this contact strategy and their areas of responsibility.
4. Provide education on all product sets for all groups and be less blinkered.
5. Provide a "telephone account manager" for high value

customers. This person would be the main interface into FSP and would know the customer's day-to-day dealings.

6. As a new product was brought on stream, each product line had created their own processes, therefore streamlining and redesigning these to evoke their desired emotions was critical.

7. The organization had only limited capability to identify high value customers when they phoned in and so these people were treated the same as everyone else. Therefore, implement a customer relationship management (CRM) system across the company and flag high value customers.

8. Identify the "best people" in the call centre and ensure that they deal with the high value customers.

9. Look to integrate offerings to make them appear seamless.

10. Undertake retraining in the call centre for emotional engagement.

11. Lay plans now and budget for the next segment and channel to be completed.

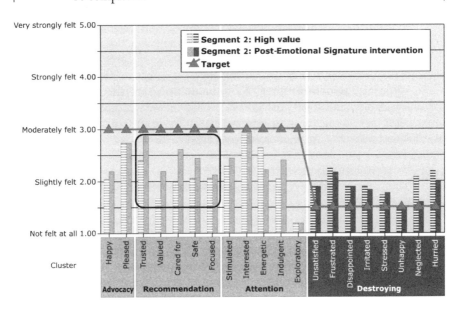

Figure 6.4 FSP: post-intervention scores

As you will see in Figure 6.4, the line shows the target they set themselves to achieve, noticably a straight line. This is not something that we would advise, but being a very target-driven organization this was the view that Gus and the team wanted to go ahead with. On running the figures through our Emotional Signature of Value model, it showed that this would achieve an additional

£18,920,000 ($34,400,000)

There were some significant costs involved like a CRM system to provide a complete view of the customer. Also the implementation of the telephone account management function had a significant cost but some of this was offset by the time saved for the f2f channel. We cannot reveal the final figure but there was still a considerable profit at the end of the year for achieving these targets.

Gus, Qaalfa and I presented this to the FSP management board. It was one of those presentations where you don't know if you are doing well or not as we were being asked so many questions on the numbers that you don't know if this is interest or skepticism. Fortunately, we were able to explain that their financial teams and marketing intelligence group had already signed off our methodology and, therefore, after some robust debate on the numbers from the CFO, he conceded that he was unable to find fault in the way the business case was reached. I remember him saying, "This is the first time I can remember that I have seen evidence of how a 'soft' function can be turned into a hard business case." Praise indeed!

In summary, remember that recommendations are the foundations of customer loyalty, and loyal customers cost less to service and thus save you money. Let us now move on to how we can move to the top of our hierarchy of value and convert customers into advocates!

Note

1. "Unlocking Customer Advocacy in Retail Banking: the Customer-focused Enterprise", S. Lieberman and R. Heffernan (2006) *Building an Edge,* the financial services newsletter,14 November, **7**(4). An IBM research study.

7 The Advocacy Cluster

There are only two organizations of which I am an advocate. The first is Virgin Atlantic. I fly to the US about 15 times a year to see clients or to go to our Atlanta office, therefore the carrier I use is important to me. I think they do an excellent job. As I travel so often I am a gold card member of the frequent flyer program. Their new lounge at Heathrow, London is great and offers a range of complimentary services, for example massages, haircuts, shoe shines and many other indulgent experiences. The whole experience has a different feel to any other airline I have traveled on and I have traveled on a lot of airlines! It feels more personalized, new, trendy, upbeat and a mixture of casual sophistication – all at the same time. But the thing that really makes it for me is the people. They do a great job of engaging with you and also of understanding if you want to talk or just unwind, when they stay out of your way.

Last year I attended an open day at a stately home for gold card members with Lorraine. The day was very well organized and included clay pigeon shooting, hot air balloon rides, and so on, along with a champagne buffet. All this was complimentary. This is important to me as I can take Lorraine which is some compensation for me being away so much.

The second organization I advocate is Disney. When the kids were young we took them to Disney on a number of occasions. Even now my kids, aged between 22 and 17, would be happy to visit and enjoy the rides. My eldest daughter, Coralie, has been to Disney Paris on three or four occasions and Lorraine and I are looking forward to taking our grandchildren there one day.

Being in the business of Customer Experience makes me sensitive to what I experience and these are the only two companies I would advocate. In fact, relating my experience to you now is a good example of what an advocate does; proactively advocates the organization to you.

The Advocacy Cluster is made up of only two emotions, *happy* and *pleased*. This should also tell you something. Because this cluster only has two statistically significant emotions, this means these emotions are really important. In fact Dr Jeremy Miles, the statistician who worked on this for us, in the beginning called this cluster the "big daddy!"

Let us just look at happiness. There are two ways of looking at this; being happy in the moment and the more holistic feeling of being in a happy "state," as we discussed in Chapter 2. You will also recall from that chapter that it is important to understand customers' "goal states" and this is what people are striving to achieve, either consciously or subconsciously. Therefore, before we look at the detail of how you can evoke happiness in your experience, let us for a moment look at the more holistic concept of being happy and at this as a goal state, as this also can impact your experience.

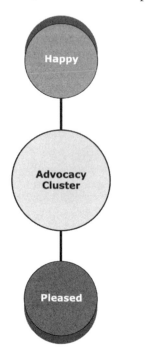

It is very common for people to strive to be happy. In fact, it is famously enshrined in the American Declaration of Independence ... "and the pursuit of Happiness." To take this more holistic view I would like you to think about a happy time. Ideally, if you can, look at a photo of a happy time, maybe of your family.

I have a photograph in my study of a family Christmas lunch some 15 years ago. Our kids, Coralie, Ben and Abbie were 7, 5 and 2 respectively. Coralie is in a party dress and is showing off a lovely bracelet, probably a Christmas present. Ben looks very smart in a waistcoat, white shirt and bow tie and is sitting on a booster seat to reach the table. Abbie is in her highchair, again in a party dress, and she has managed to plaster food all over herself and most of the surrounding area! As I stared at the photo I was transported back to those happy times and the memories came flooding back to me. I am sure it is the same for you.

Figure 7.1 Advocacy Cluster

Our memories have strong links to our emotions. Just take a moment and look at your picture. Is the picture of your partner, your kids, your parents, your pet or maybe your friends? Or possibly a great Customer Experience you have had with your bank? I think not!

It is interesting that I don't remember the bad times so much, with the kids, the arguments, when they woke at night or changing the diapers (nappies). It's also interesting that we don't have photographs of the bad times; we only take them of good events. You can imagine it, in the middle of an argument, saying "Great, can everyone just stay where you are as I want to capture this moment for the family album!" When you peel back the onion we all crave happiness. This is one of the reasons we take these pictures of happy moments, to extend our feelings and help us remember that moment, so we can revisit that time and feel those emotions again.

Humans have strived to be happy for thousands of years, but what this means to you may be different to what it means for someone else.

People say, "Maybe if I didn't work as much and had a job without so much responsibility it would make me happy?" or "If only I had a vacation home I would be happy" or "If I had what they have I would be happy."

But as many people will tell you, money doesn't buy you happiness. It was interesting to read in a study of lottery winners that after the initial joy of winning they all reverted to their original levels of happiness.

Ask yourself this. If you were to take a photo of yourself today and then look back at it in five years' time, would you say you were happy? According to the latest research, most of us would probably say we are still striving to be happy. In Richard Layard's book *Happiness*, he uses a well-published statistic and informs us:

> In UK, America and Japan, on average, people are no happier today than people were 50 years ago. Yet, at the same time, average incomes have more than doubled in the USA, UK and Japan.[1]

Therefore people are striving for things to make them happy. Can your Customer Experience be one of them? There is a growing body of experts looking into happiness as a subject and investigating its impact, or not, on societies around the world. This has spawned a new branch of psychology called "positive psychology" founded by Professor Martin Seligman, whose research demonstrates that it is possible to be happier, and feel more satisfied, regardless of one's circumstances. The growth in popularity of this subject and its fascinating results were reported in a six-part TV series aired by the BBC in the UK called *The Happiness Factor*. The BBC website states:

> Britain is less happy than in the 1950s – despite the fact that we are three times richer. The proportion of people saying they are "very happy" has fallen from 52% in 1957 to just 36% today. The British experience mirrors data from America, where social scientists have seen levels of life satisfaction gradually decline over the last quarter of a century.[2]

Layard, Seligman and also Professor Daniel Kahneman of the University of Princeton (a winner of the Nobel Prize on the subject) tell us that it is not money that brings you happiness. In fact the evidence suggests that once you have reached an average income of about £10,000 ($18,000), your happiness levels do not rise much further. So if it is not money, what is it and how can your organization contribute?

Further research was conducted for the BBC[3] which revealed the following interesting statistics:

- In almost every developed country, happiness levels have remained largely static over the past 50 years – despite huge increases in income.
- Compared to 22% of people who said their neighborhood was friendlier than 10 years ago, 43% said their neighborhood was less friendly.
- Almost half of people – 48% – say that relationships are the biggest factor in making them happy. Second is health at 24%.
- When asked whether the government's prime objective should be the greatest happiness or the greatest wealth, a remarkable 81% stated they wanted happiness as the goal; only 13% wanted greatest wealth.

- Marriage also seems to be very important. According to research, the effect of a happy marriage adds an average of seven years to the life of a man and approximately four years for a woman.

Our happiness can even affect our life expectancy. In a well-known study of the "Sisters of Notre Dame" (a group of nuns from Milwaukee), scientists were asked to read the diaries the nuns had kept since the 1930s. The scientists then categorized the nuns into whether they believed they were happy or not, based on their writings. The important aspect of this study is that clearly nuns have a similar lifestyle to each other, their living conditions are the same, their routine is the same, the food is the same, and so on. The fascinating finding is the "happy" nuns seemed to live nine years longer than the "unhappy" nuns – an amazing finding. This is particularly interesting when you consider the focus and research on smoking and obesity by governments, from which they now estimate that smoking takes three years off your life expectancy. This is in comparison to nine years for being "happy," which maybe shows a new focus is needed! As it is also believed that happier people are healthier in general and more resistant to illness, maybe the goal of government should be to make citizens happier and thus increase life expectancy.

So what has all this got to do with the Customer Experience? Well simply this. You need to realize that happiness is important to your customers, and in the main, they are probably striving to be happy as an overall goal state, either consciously or subconsciously. Surely if this is the case, then wouldn't it be a good idea if your organization tried to help them achieve this and provide a good experience rather than just treat them as a transaction? Surely, as the research illustrates that "relationships" are one of the key contributors to making people feel happy, it would be a good idea for you to build that relationship with customers into your experience rather than employing people who couldn't care less. Furthermore, with this growing weight of evidence, you should be designing a "deliberate" Customer Experience that evokes happiness to help customers in their quest.

For our part, to support this evidence, we know that the Advocacy Cluster of emotions, *happy* and *pleased*, creates loyal customers and is further evidence of the importance of happiness. However, we also know that most customers would not describe their Customer Experiences as "happy."

In our view, our aim must be to evoke the Advocacy Cluster of emotions and in so doing provide a happy experience that customers would want to take a picture of. Maybe this is a good test. Ask yourself:

Is your Customer Experience good enough that your customers want to take a picture of it?

If the answer is no, we have some work to do. This is our challenge.

As people crave happiness, what we need to do is give them little "fixes" or treats by designing them into your experience. This brings us to the second way to look at this cluster – creating a number of events that make the customer feel happy or pleased.

It's funny, when you start to recall a Customer Experience that has made you happy, it's quite difficult. If you do think of one, then you have probably thought of a vacation, a day out to a theme park or some form of entertainment. But do you remember feeling "happy" when you had an experience with your bank, your utility provider or your local DIY shop? These aren't frequent. Maybe you felt happy or pleased when the bank manager said "yes" to your mortgage application and this meant you could buy your new house. These occasions are "event" led. What we mean by this is there are events that lend themselves to providing a happy experience, such as a celebration, a wedding, an anniversary party, a graduation, a birthday, or Christmas lunch at a restaurant. There are also everyday experiences where we are trying to get that "fix" of the Advocacy Cluster of emotions: a trip to the theatre, a night out at a restaurant with friends, a visit to the movies. All these events can make us happy while they last, but then our feelings revert back to normal. In these sectors of business, it is easier to evoke these emotions. The challenge comes when you are trying to create a happy and pleased experience with car rental or in the B2B market – it is not impossible, just more difficult.

As before, let's look at both of these emotions in more depth.

Happy

Definition: To feel good; a state of contented joy; cheerful, a positive state of mind; a feeling showing or causing pleasure and enjoyment.

As we discussed in previous chapters, if you feel happy, then you have typically passed through a number of the emotions like valued, cared for, stimulated, and so on. For some, cared for or valued can evoke happiness, for others "interested" or "stimulated" can have the same effect, dependent on the circumstances. What we certainly know is that the destroying emotions do not make people happy. Chuck Kavitsky, CEO of Fireman's Fund Insurance Company, and his team understand the correlation between these emotions:

> The normal problem that comes when you start doing things differently is that it costs money. However we don't look at it that way. We look at it as doing those special things that are emotionally engaging, these are good for business and ultimately sell your policies. If your policyholders and agents know that you are going to "value" them and "care for" them and endeavor to make them "happy" then you're going to breed loyalty. It becomes less of an issue of price and more an issue of value. We believe there is room for a company with this kind of different attitude, that this emotional engagement separates us from others.

Emotions are a key differentiator. Clearly, understanding what makes a customer feel happy is therefore significant, both from a physical and emotional perspective. Then, of course, you have to plan to deliver it. A great example and exponent of this is Disney:

> We conduct private and public "best practice study tours" in London and Los Angeles when we take delegates on "behind the scenes tours" of a number of companies. One of these organizations is Disney. They proudly inform our delegates that the stated aim of their experience is to make customers happy. To achieve this they have undertaken a great deal of detailed research, and continue to do so, of what will make their customers happy from a physical and emotional point of view.
>
> For example, they realized early on that the lines for the rides would be a problem. Therefore they have made standing in a line entertaining by having lots of activities going on, with lots of attention to detail. Typically, they will inform you of the queue time and try to overestimate the time, so when you get through quicker you are pleased. Also to help with this challenge they introduced their "fast pass" system to reduce wait times.
>
> They know their customers like a clean and happy environment. They therefore play music appropriate to the occasion or location, happy music as you come in, more somber music as you leave, tired after a hard day. They know that our senses are linked directly to emotions. In their experience design, they place popcorn at strategic points in the park. They know that the smell of popcorn evokes positive feelings, like going to the movies when you were a child. They place coffee stalls strategically for the smell to waft around the park in the morning. As you can imagine with all the gifts, sweets, popcorn, ice cream and such like, trash can become a big issue. Their research shows that cleanliness has an impact on the experience of the guest. From their research, they know that a guest will only carry a piece of trash for about 15 paces before they drop it on the floor. Knowing this, you will see a trash bin, on average every 12 paces. This, then, helps in providing a great experience but also saves costs on not employing so many sweepers.

All these individual actions contribute to the customer feeling happy. Here is the view of Maxine Clark, CEO Build-A-Bear Workshop:

> If they're buying for themselves, we ask: "Is this for you?" "Oh great, is it a special occasion that you're treating yourself today?" "No I just wanted to have a fun day." "OK, have you been to a Build-A-Bear Workshop store before?" "No I haven't been here before." "Well, what kind of animals do you like?" and then you get into that conversation. Then, when they are stuffing the animal and they make a wish, that's the great magical moment and evokes emotions like stimulation, energetic and happy in our customers. We try to make everyone happy. We don't treat a 16-year-old the same way we treat a 6-year-old. Sometimes 16-year-olds are very conscious of how they are acting in public; they may not want to jump around and kiss the heart, whereas younger children love to do that, that's part of the fun of it. So we try to make sure that we capture that magical moment, but age grade it, if you will.
>
> One of the greatest compliments I hear about Build-A-Bear Workshop is no matter what store they go into the people are so friendly! They ask how we hire and train that high level of service. It's really quite simple, we hire people who care. That's something you can't really teach. We do have a structured training program, but what it really

comes down to is we have a small manual with one big word in it … YES. There is nothing your Guests are going to ask you that is going to put you out of business. Can I use your phone? Do you have a restroom? Can I exchange this for another size? All simple questions that cause big stirs in some companies … but it's just that easy … say YES. We want to be a place where people are happy.

All these actions show Build-A-Bear customers that they are cared for, and make guests happy.

Typical actions you can take to evoke "happy" in a Customer Experience are:

- Understand the holistic picture of the customer
- Build a relationship with the customer
- Be friendly to the customer
- Consistently evoke the Attention and Recommendation Clusters of emotions
- Have a clear understanding of your customer's physical and emotional expectations and plan to exceed them
- Look for something outside the norm
- Plan and execute a "deliberate" and consistent Customer Experience.

A "not very happy" experience

A mother is helping to organize her daughter's wedding. She has agreed to be responsible for arranging the hotel reception. Having just been divorced, she has moved to another part of the country and is now a two-hour drive from the hotel. While she cannot criticize the hotel for anything, they seem to be just doing what they are asked. It feels to the mother that she is driving all the decisions and clearly she wants to make the day very special for her daughter. On the day, the staff, in the main, do what they are expected to do but look like they are going through the motions. This forces the mother to constantly check everything is happening as she expects and as a result she doesn't enjoy her day because of this. On reflection, at the end of the day, the mother is disappointed as she felt the day was bland and it could have been better.

How this could be converted to a happy experience

From their very first meeting, the banqueting manager at the hotel couldn't be more helpful. He was particularly empathetic when he found out the mother was recently divorced and now lives away from the area. He knows this is a special day for both the bride and groom, but also the mother, particularly due to these circumstances. He is very proactive with suggestions of how to make the day special and even goes so far as to suggest seating arrangements. To be of further help, he takes photographs of other weddings so the mother can decide where to locate the gift table, the wedding cake and how to decorate the venue. He then emails the suggestions to the mother as he knows she is some distance away but wants to ensure it is a perfect day. On the day of the wedding, the banqueting manager and his people are very attentive. They add a few extra touches that the mother was unaware of, for instance they escort the top table to dinner. After the event, the banqueting manager collects a series of mementoes of the event, champagne corks, invitation cards, and so on and posts them to the mother with a card from all the staff at the hotel saying congratulations for organizing a great event!

Clearly, the mother's memories would have been very different to those in the first scenario and would then initiate recommendation or advocacy.

Pleased

Definition: very satisfied, the feeling when something good has been achieved or has happened to you; a state of heightened satisfaction.

Feeling pleased is above satisfaction. If you feel satisfied, you have got what you expected. However, if you are feeling pleased, you have progressed one step further. It could be that you have been pleased to finally finish the Christmas shopping, that you are pleased your new car has been delivered. Feeling "pleased" is on its way to being happy, but not quite there. Typically, you will see people smile and you have a feeling of satisfaction and contentment.

For a number of years now Lorraine and I have banked with First Direct, a telephone and internet bank in the UK. They are part of the HSBC group and are renowned for their great experience. As I started to write this part of the book I asked Lorraine why she was so pleased with their service. Here was her reply:

> They answer the phone quickly and it's by a person and not a voice menu system. They introduce themselves, are always polite and keen to help. The really great thing is they know what they are talking about and they don't waffle but get straight to the point. The people have always been very friendly and do not force themselves on you. Offering 24/7 telephone banking and a great, manageable internet site means I can manage our money very efficiently; so much so that we now have more than one account with them including our mortgage and a few other services.

This is fairly typical of a committed advocate of their service. Taken from the dooyoo.co.uk comparison website, this review of First Direct comes from a user called "annalovesworks":

> I can't sing the praises of First Direct highly enough, and I can't recommend them fast

enough. Back in 1996 I was reluctant to move my bank account from NatWest, as I had been banking with them for about 7 years; I thought it would be a hassle. But then NatWest changed the way I could get in contact with them (I couldn't call my branch direct any more), and I heard wonderful things about First Direct – how you could phone them at any time to set up Standing Orders or cancel them, or move money around – and it all happened in minutes.

I moved my account; in the end it was so simple to do it, and I haven't had a moment of regret. In fact the Customer Service is SO fantastic that I have even had a few laughs with the telephone operators over the years; even if I am just calling up to check a balance the call is always a nice experience (even if it turns out I'm in the red!).

I have subsequently set up a Joint Account with First Direct, my partner has set up a Cheque Account with them, we have taken loans out with them, a savings account, ISAs and some travel and household insurance. I think I might be going First Direct crazy. But it's just so easy to deal with them, and, touch wood, they always get it right. :)

In both these examples, I would suggest that First Direct have evoked the feeling of being pleased.

In 2006, I was presenting at the UK Customer Management conference in Edinburgh with Chris Pilling, the CEO for First Direct. I got the chance to tell him what a good job they were doing. During his presentation he shared some interesting facts about First Direct:

- A new customer is recommended to them every five seconds!
- 86% of customers have recommended someone in the past three months
- This saves £150 ($270) per person in acquisition costs
- 92% of their customers are extremely, or very satisfied with them
- Staff attrition is half that of other industries.

But there was one chart in Chris's presentation that amazed me. Chris was showing a chart of customer satisfaction with their ATMs. Most UK banks were at about the same rate, varying between 65–70% satisfaction. First Direct was at 89%. The really fascinating thing here is that First Direct do not have any ATMs! As part of the HSBC group, customers use ATMs that are branded HSBC (and obviously other banks' ATMs). Having said this, First Direct customers *think* that First Direct ATMs are much better! This is because of the great experience they have, thus, as we indicated in Chapter 2, "Be careful what you look for because you'll find it." As First Direct customers are advocates, they also advocate things they don't even have! They look at everything and think it is positive!

Typical actions you can take to evoke "pleased" in a Customer Experience are:

- First fix your destroying emotions
- Start to evoke the Attention and Advocacy Clusters of emotions.
- Have a clear understanding of your customers' physical and emotional expectations

- Measure so that customer expectations are met as a minimum
- Consider the extra "nice" touches you can do for a customer
- Really look at the detail of your Customer Experience
- Provide an empathetic Customer Experience.

A not very pleasing experience

A couple want a specific room in a hotel as this was the room they stayed in on their honeymoon 10 years ago. The room is provided for them but the check-in is just like any other transaction. No mention is made of the anniversary by anyone from the hotel. Nothing happens!

How this can be changed to a pleasing Customer Experience

A couple want a specific room in a hotel as this was the room they stayed in on their honeymoon 10 years ago. The hotel books them the room and sends directions of how to get there. When they check in, they are welcomed back to the hotel and told that the room they selected is ready; the receptionist congratulates them on their 10-year anniversary. There is a bottle of champagne in the room and a card from the manager congratulating them on their wedding anniversary, as well as a copy of the newspaper from that day 10 years ago. When they go down for a meal in the evening, the management has selected a special table with a view over the lake, placed some extra candles on the table and they deliver a small wedding cake. A few days after returning home, the couple receive an invitation to visit the hotel on their next anniversary at a discount rate.

This example describes both happy and pleased as part of the Advocacy Cluster. Let's now go on to put this together for you in a case study of an airline we dealt with who focused on these two emotions, particularly for their high value business class customers. For reasons of confidentiality, we will call them World Airlines.

Case study: World Airlines (WA)

World Airlines (WA) have been in the market for a number of years and have had an excellent track record for providing a good customer service, especially for their business class passengers. They provide services to most major cities in the world but also have a focus on the lucrative Europe to USA market for business travelers. When they started, they were seen as ground-breaking in a number of areas; however, over the years this has worn off and the board were increasingly worried that they were losing their differentiator.

On the face of it their world looked fine. Revenue was still growing but not as much as in the past, even after taking into account the effect of 9/11. Most concerning to them was that their customer satisfaction was on a steady decline and had been for the past 10 months, which is worrying for an organization that prides themselves on their customer service.

We were called in by John, VP of customer services, who knew of our work from another client who had recommended us. In the past, WA had designed some innovative experiences that had raised the bar significantly for other carriers. However, this was now a different market. With 9/11 and subsequent security challenges, it appeared they had taken their eye off the ball. They had been trying to improve the security experience, so it would not have so much impact on the passengers, a laudable aim, as we know that the emotion of "safe" in the Recommendation Cluster is fundamental. As you will see from the figures below, they were doing as well as any other airline. Most concerning was that their high margin business class service particularly had seen a downturn.

On the first week of our engagement, we also discovered that they were focused on more of the physical aspects of their experience, such as:

- On-time departures
- Check-in procedure
- Quality and availability of the duty free service
- Professionalism of the crew
- The value of the flight
- The selection of movies
- The quality of food.

We also reviewed their latest customer satisfaction data. The first thing we noticed was that there was virtually no emotional measurement. We spent time studying the data and looking for the reasons behind their decline. We decided to run some focus groups to get direct feedback from customers. Their headline message was "WA seems to have lost their edge." It certainly appeared that things weren't as before. Some frequent flyers we interviewed also admitted that they had started to fly with some of WA's competitors "just to see what they were like." I remember one of the passengers saying it in such a way that he was apologizing for being disloyal. This nuance was not picked up in their standard physically based survey.

After we were halfway through our engagement and at a meeting to give John and his team an update on the focus groups, he was called out urgently by the CEO, Max. The latest customer satisfaction data was in – another decline. Max was now officially worried. John returned to the meeting, a bit ashen-faced. I gather being reprimanded by Max was not a pleasant experience! I was empathetic to John's situation and decided to adjourn the meeting so that he could gather his thoughts. I suggested John and I went for a walk outside. It turned out that Max had threatened that John would lose his job if he didn't get this fixed. John said he knew this was a lot of hot air and he had a number of months before that would happen, as he knew Max quite well and it was just a spur of the moment reprimand. However, his parting words to me as we went back to the meeting were, "We need to get this sorted Colin, otherwise Max will be very serious next time." We went back into the room; John was very professional and we had a good debate on the findings.

The next stage was to undertake the Emotional Signature survey with the same people who had just completed their standard survey. We explained that WA were measuring the physical aspects of the experience and, as over 50% of the Customer Experience was about emotions, they were only getting half the story. We felt strongly that our survey would give them another view of what was happening.

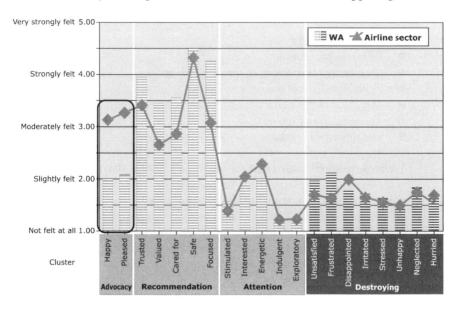

Figure 7.2 WA: pre-intervention scores

You will see the first survey results in Figure 7.2. You can see that they are doing well in most of the clusters compared to the rest of the airline sector. However, the Destroying Cluster is higher than we would have liked to see for an organization that prides itself on service. Also you will see the Advocacy Cluster was disproportionately lower than the other sectors. This supported our findings from the focus groups. Over the next three months we ran the two surveys side by side.

The combination of both results showed us that they still had a group of loyal customers who gave them a high score on their standard, physical survey. These people were reporting a high level of satisfaction on the Emotional Signature (ES) survey, particularly in the Advocacy Cluster of emotions. These customers also spent the most.

We were able to show that an increasing number of customers were giving only a slightly lower score on their standard physical survey, but when you looked at the Emotional Signature results of this group, there was a marked difference in their advocacy scores. They were not as happy or pleased with the service as they had been a year ago; they were also spending less and using other carriers.

We discovered that WA had mistakenly thought that the declining customer satisfaction measure was because customers thought they were providing a worse physical service. This was not the case; they were not sufficiently emotionally engaged. We saw that an increase in the destroyers was typical of a loss of emotional engagement with customers. From here, customers would start to see other things that were wrong. As they were losing the happy and pleased aspects of the service, they were also "picking holes" in the normal service and this was coming through in the measures. Ironically, the normal measures would not uncover this.

This means that WA were wasting resources trying to fix things that, in effect, weren't really problems. In addition, when you started to look at the experience from an emotional perspective, you could find examples in the areas where they were providing a poor experience.

For example, we undertook a Customer Mirror, using concealed video cameras recording the interactions between staff and customers, during a time of "increased security alert," meaning the ground staff were asked to work much longer hours to get passengers through the system. On one video we saw check-in staff complaining to customers how this delay was causing them a personal problem! Also we went through the lost baggage procedure, a highly emotional interaction. We discovered that on calling the lost baggage call centre on a number of occasions, over a few days, a voice message would say: "Due to high call volumes, please call back later." We told John and the team that from the customer perspective this meant one of two things; either, they couldn't answer the calls as they didn't have enough people, or they were losing lots of bags!

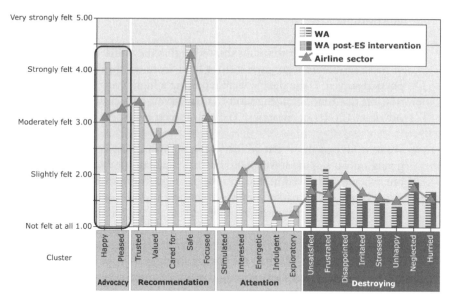

Figure 7.3 WA: pre- vs post-intervention scores

Armed with this data, we conducted a series of workshops and defined new targets for the changes that were needed. In Figure 7.3 you will see the outcome of their work in this snapshot of their new measurement system. Our recommendations were as follows:

1. Implement Emotional Signature as an ongoing measurement.
2. Focus attention back on the Customer Experience and if necessary employ additional staff.
3. Relaunch the emotional side of the Customer Experience with employees.
4. Define new services for their high value customers.
5. Retrain the business class cabin crew on what they need to do to make the journey a happy and pleasing Customer Experience.
6. Put more time and effort into innovation from an emotional perspective and build this into a newly designed experience.
7. Redesign the main business class lounge.
8. Provide additional concierge services to business class passengers.
9. Focus on winning back the frequent flyers, who had started to move to other airlines, with offers of discounted flights in order to demonstrate the new level of service.

This combined with the targets showed that they would generate additional revenue of

£23,650,000 ($43,000,000)

These recommendations were then fully costed and a business case was presented to the board. Nearly all the recommendations were accepted. They have been conducting the Emotional Signature for a while now and the combination of the physical and emotional measures have again revealed many areas they would not have understood without considering both aspects of the experience.

We have now described all the clusters that drive and destroy value. We hope this gives you a good understanding of what can be achieved. If not, feel free to email at contact@beyondphilsophy.com or visit our website at www.beyondphilsophy.com. Let's now see how these can be used in a new measure, the Net Promoter® Score.

Notes

1. *Happiness: Lessons from a New Science*, Layard, R. (2006) Harmondsworth, Penguin.
2. news.bbc.co.uk/1/hi/programmes/happiness_formula/4771908.stm.
3. Conducted by GfK NOP for the BBC – news.bbc.co.uk/nol/shared/bsp/hi/pdfs/29_03_06_happiness_gfkpoll.pdf.

8 The Link to Financial Performance via Net Promoter® Score

There are many businesses now investigating and using a new customer measure, Net Promoter® Score (NPS) and rightly so, as we believe this is a very good measure. However, once an organization has understood their NPS, we have been asked on a number of occasions "what should we do now?" NPS gives you a great top level view but needs some granularity to make the changes necessary to improve your score. In our experience some of these changes are physical, some emotional. Therefore, in its very construction, we have ensured that the Emotional Signature links directly to NPS so that these tools can be used together. This is exciting as it allows us to tap into the growing body of research on the link between NPS and financial performance. Qaalfa Dibeehi is our vice president of consulting and thought leadership and, as such, one of the key people, along with Steven Walden, our head of research, who has developed Emotional Signature. Qaalfa has gone on to specialize in NPS and its links to the Emotional Signature. Therefore it seems most appropriate that we let him explain how they complement each other and, moreover, how together they can be used as a powerful tool to improve your Customer Experience.

I have been fortunate enough to have lived and worked in three of the world's premier destination cities: New York City, Tokyo and now London. While they each share their big city commonalities, they are very different to me and each has its little treasures. When friends are about to visit one of these places, they often ask me for an insider's view of each city and, more importantly, an insider's recommendation of "must sees." Essentially, they are asking for a recommendation beyond what they can read in any given tourist guide.

Just last week, my friend Christa asked me what she should see while in Tokyo. My response was immediate and has not changed in almost 10 years. I said to her:

> You must go to this little jazz club in north Tokyo close to Ueno station just off Asakus-adori. You'll have to get help from a local to find it but it is worth it. I have never been to another place like it. You walk in and there are maybe 15 two-seater tables with plush, comfortable chairs and some lounge chairs. At first you will not notice anything special except that it's dim. The waiter will come over and here's where it starts to get interesting – he won't say a word. If you attempt to tell him what you want, he'll point to the rules. Number one is no talking; this is a listening club for jazz aficionados. You simply write your order on a napkin. Then you look around and there really is no talking,

anywhere! Neither the staff nor customers talk. Then you pay attention to the walls. From floor to ceiling they are lined with albums, that's the old vinyl albums, not a CD in sight. They have a full jazz library. You simply think of a tune or an artist you have not heard in ages, even obscure material, walk over to the wall, pull it out and hand it to the DJ. He'll play it. The sound system is amazing. You can hear every plucked string and swoosh of a drummer's arm. It's fantastic! The vibe is very artsy Tokyo, cutting-edge retro and a definite must see.

What's interesting is that even when I know someone isn't really into jazz, I still recommend the place because I believe they just won't find anything like it anywhere else and it really does represent a quirky side of Tokyo that the average person does not get to see.

I am sure if we took an Emotional Signature of this place they'd get very high Attention Cluster scores, and from jazz lovers, high Advocacy Cluster scores as well. On the other hand, if you are the type who can't understand why anyone would go to a place that does not allow talking, then you and others like you score this place high on the Destroying Cluster of emotions. In effect this would mean you would not visit again and you would tell other like-minded people not to visit, thus helping to preserve the special atmosphere of the place.

I have not lived in Tokyo for over 10 years but in that time I have easily sent over 100 people (mostly native Japanese) to that little club. To be honest I discovered the club only a few months before I left Tokyo for New York City. So let's say I actually went to the club only four times before I moved back to NYC and bought two $5 drinks each time. I'd represent $40 (4 × $10) (£22) in direct revenue to the club. However, let's also assume that the 100 people I sent to the club since then also bought two $5 (£2.75) drinks and furthermore let's assume that 10% of those recommended it again. Based on all the people I've influenced, I'd represent an additional $10,000 (100 × 10 × $10) (£5,500) to the club and I am not finished recommending it yet!

The point I am making is that there is an obvious interconnection between an emotionally engaging experience, the strength and duration of resultant recommendations, and revenue generation. As my story demonstrates, customer experience really gets at that long-term sustainable value based on true loyalty (that is, attitudinal loyalty that can be measured by a customer's willingness to recommend). NPS is a measure that is based on customers' willingness to recommend a business and it has been shown to correlate with revenue growth. From a customer-centric perspective, revenue growth can stem from any combination of four types of value. Let's explore these types of value before we tackle NPS in earnest.

Types of value

Among the different types of potential value that a business can go after, one thing is common to them all, they are founded ultimately on the behavior of customers that results in revenue gains over time. In particular, four types of value are key to long-term revenue growth (Figure 8.1):

■ *Extrapolated value* – the additional revenue that results as an individual customer chooses to continue to do business with a company over time. Extrapolated value is what many businesses refer to when they speak of loyalty – the customer continues to come back. The act of coming back is behavioral loyalty. Attitudinal loyalty implies coming back even when it's not convenient. Interestingly, by this definition alone, I would not be considered a loyal customer of that Tokyo jazz club even though I have consistently driven business their way.

■ *Incremental value* – the additional revenue that results from an individual customer spending more per transaction on average than they have in the past. Increasing incremental value represents gains in share of wallet. So for example, if a given customer has £100 ($180) in her wallet to spend, the incremental value equates to the capture of a larger share of that £100 for the business.

■ *Strategic value* – the additional revenue that results from an individual customer buying a company's other goods and services. This type of value is what is sought from cross-selling, for instance when companies embark on a program of brand extension and stretching.[1] However, cross-selling requires the customer to give a business the benefit of the doubt that its goods or services will meet their expectation in some area not traditionally associated with the company. An example is when a customer chooses to buy a company's "widgets" even though they know the company best for its "gizmos."

■ *Social network value* – the additional revenue that results from an individual customer influencing others to buy from a particular business. Social network value refers to viral spend. More specifically, it refers to a person's ability to actively initiate viral spend – influencing others to behave commercially in a similar fashion. My social network value to the little Tokyo jazz club is impressive, even if I do say so myself.

Thus, *potential value* is the summation of possible future extrapolated, incremental, strategic and social network (EISS) value. In contrast, *customer value* is the summation of EISS value at a point in time. *Historic value* is the summation of EISS to date. As customer *lifetime value* is the summation of current and potential value, it becomes clear that it is possible to affect customer potential or lifetime value by changing any of the EISS values. Up to now, most large corporations have addressed their customer-oriented strategy via programs like customer relationship management (CRM) in an attempt to increase extrapolated, incremental and strategic value, and the use of a customer satisfaction measurement program.

CRM was the start of the customer focus as a strategic imperative and popularized the notion that the company should attempt to see and treat its valuable customers as individuals. However, in order to do so, it required companies to recognize who the valuable customers were and what it was they wanted. Unfortunately, most of what was talked about in CRM was customers' rational/ physical expectations. Customer Experience has taken up where CRM left off and expanded upon it.

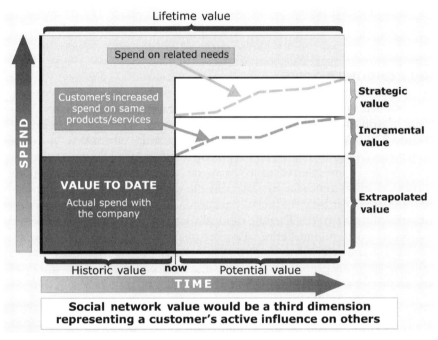

Figure 8.1 Types of value (adapted from Richard Sheahan, Counterpoint3)

As the customer-focused strategic imperative became accepted, the use of customer satisfaction as a key performance indicator (KPI) became prevalent. However, customer satisfaction was soon found not to be very strongly linked to the basic customer behavior that business was interested in – chief among these is behavior that leads to extrapolated value (that is, loyalty). It is now known that high customer satisfaction is not necessarily associated with high customer loyalty.[2] In other words, customers who are known to be satisfied can leave just as easily as customers who are unsatisfied. This posed a problem for customer centricity proponents. The answer came on the back of further research suggesting that the Customer Experience is not only composed of the rational elements that customer satisfaction tends to get at, but also emotional elements that it does not cover. Furthermore, the emotional experience is now thought to account for at least half the entire Customer Experience. A new measurement was required – one which was sensitive to the entire Customer Experience and especially the emotional part.

As stated earlier, the Customer Experience encompasses both physical and emotional components and recognizes that it is the traditionally hard-to-assess emotional component that drives much of our behavior.

Successful forward-thinking organizations are beginning to understand, therefore, that the Customer Experience is linked to the full EISS value (that is, including social network value) and thus are hungry for a measure of value that is more sensitive and accurate than customer satisfaction and, importantly, shown to be related to financial performance. One measure increasingly being adopted by businesses that meets both these criteria is Net Promoter® Score (NPS).

Net Promoter® Score

NPS is calculated on the basis of customers' answers to the question "How likely are you to recommend (a company, product or experience) to a friend?" (Figure 8.2). Customers answer on a 10-point scale, where 0 is "not at all likely to recommend" and 10 is "very likely to recommend." Those customers who rate 9–10 are referred to as *Promoters*. These customers are loyal and encourage others to behave commercially the way they do; only Promoters can be considered positively emotionally engaged. The customers who answer 7–8 are referred to as *Passives*. They are rationally satisfied but can be easily taken by competitors with minimal effort; Passives are emotionally neutral. Those who answer 1–6 are referred to as *Detractors*. Detractors are essentially trapped customers who are expected to leave the first chance they get; at worst they are negatively emotionally engaged.

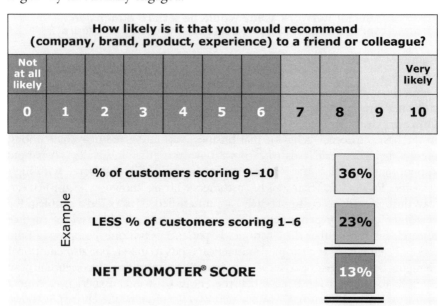

Figure 8.2 Net Promoter® Score calculation

The Net Promoter® Score is calculated as the percentage of Promoters minus the percentage of Detractors. Immediately, we see that it is much easier for a customer to score in the Detractor range than the Promoter range. Thus, a business has to put in extra effort to ensure that customers are closer to saying that they are "very likely to recommend" the business. Also, notice that the NPS can be negative when the percentage of customers who are Detractors is greater than the percentage of customers who are Promoters.

NPS was developed by Dr. Laura Brooks, director of research at Satmetrix, and Fred Reichheld, the recognized expert on loyalty and fellow at Bain & Co. They studied a variety of potential measures and found that "likelihood to recommend" was best correlated with consumers' behavioral changes over time.

Reichheld and his colleagues at Bain have been particularly interested in understanding the relationship between NPS and financial performance. They and others continue to publish findings that verify and validate the link between NPS and financial performance, especially a firm's revenue growth.

Reichheld in particular has driven the popularization of NPS with board-level executives through his publications, especially his *Harvard Business Review* article and more recently his book *The Ultimate Question: Driving Good Profits and True Growth*.[3] When I was debating this with her, Laura Brooks stated that "the adoption of NPS isn't coming from the market research community; it's coming from the CEO who is passing it down through the organization." It is being adopted as a strategic KPI, not simply as a tactical project measure.

Net Promoter® Score and revenue growth

It is the strength of the relationship between NPS and revenue growth that has captivated these board-level executives. Reichheld has found that companies that are NPS leaders outgrow their competitors in most industries by an average of 2.5 times. In the 2005 London School of Economics advocacy–growth study, Marsden et al.[4] found that NPS is a statistically significant predictor of annual sales growth (based on a sample of 1,256 adult consumers). Indeed, Marsden found that a 7-point increase in NPS correlated with a 1% increase in growth (1-point increase = 0.147% more growth) whereas a 1% reduction in negative word of mouth led to just under 1% growth (a 1% reduction = 0.414% more growth).

In our research based on 1,109 adult customers (both B2C and B2B), we found that each of the emotion clusters – the three value driver clusters (Attention, Recommendation and Advocacy) and the Destroying Cluster – are found to be independently related to "likelihood to recommend." This means that we are able to predict the gain in revenue growth that can be expected as a result of changes in the Emotional Signature scores. While the connection would seem to be straightforward, we have discovered an important intervening relationship between age and NPS in our own data (Figure 8.3).

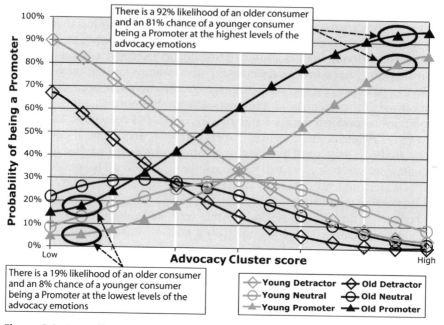

Figure 8.3 Age effect on NPS: Advocacy Cluster example

Unexpectedly, for a given emotional cluster, older consumers are more likely to be Promoters than younger consumers! For example, at the highest levels along the Advocacy Cluster of emotions, older consumers are 92% likely to be a Promoter versus only 81% for a younger consumer. At the lowest levels of the Advocacy Cluster of emotions, older consumers are 19% likely to be a Promoter, whereas it's only 8% for younger consumers. Similar patterns are displayed in each of the emotion clusters. In other words, an older customer base is on the whole more likely to be Promoters than a younger customer base, regardless of the Emotional Signature. I suppose you could call this the cynical factor as much as you can the age factor. The finding may suggest that younger consumers are more cynical than older consumers. They are more sensitive to insincere ulterior motives, even if the experience they receive is positive. This finding is in line with the fact that young consumers are harder to reach, especially if your business is considered "uncool." In Customer Experience terms, it means that it will be more difficult to provide an experience that resonates with younger consumers and that they are likely to recommend. As a result of this finding, we temper the benefits predicted by an Emotional Signature to account for the age effect.

We are also able to calculate an estimated NPS given a particular Emotional Signature. Intuitively, you would expect to find the Emotional Signature of Promoters displaying relatively high average value driver scores and relatively low value destroying scores. The opposite would be expected of Detractors. The conclusion here is that understanding the Emotional Signature can help you understand what you need to change in order to achieve positive NPS status with your customers. It allows us to compare the Emotional Signature of Promoters of your business with that of your Detractors (Figure 8.4). We could then pinpoint what it is about the emotional experience of your Detractors that needs to be addressed.

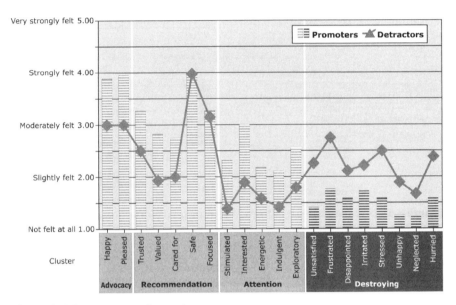

Figure 8.4 Promoters vs Detractors

Imagine a situation where your satisfaction scores are pretty good and you are not getting inordinate amounts of negative feedback – your prices are competitive and your service is on a par with your competitors. However, your churn rates are steady and not decreasing. You run a Promoter/Detractor Emotional Signature for your most valuable customers. Naturally, you expect the Promoters to score better than the Detractors. We've run across a similar situation with a B2B professional service provider. In the example below (Figure 8.5), Promoters attained 67% of the maximum advocacy score compared to 66% for Detractors.[5] The biggest difference between the Promoters and the Detractors is in the Recommendation Cluster of emotions, where Promoters attained 75% of the maximum rating possible versus only 62% for the Detractors. Thus, the advice would be for this company to focus on the Recommendation Cluster of emotions with their Detractor valuable customers in an effort to convert them to Promoters.

Thus, Emotional Signature provides a method for businesses to investigate where they need to improve their Customer Experience to drive more Promoter behavior among their customers. Success in moving NPS has been shown to relate directly to increased revenue growth. The relationship between Emotional Signature, NPS and revenue growth means that business leaders

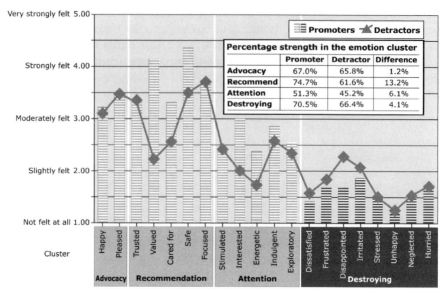

Figure 8.5 Example Promoter/Detractor Emotional Signature analysis

Table 8.1 Typical questions and answers

Key questions	Solution
What other customer measure can we use? Our satisfaction scores are fine but we continue to lose customers	Institute Net Promoter® Score as a key measure
What do we need to focus on to improve our Net Promoter® Score?	Compare the emotional signature of your company versus the competitor that customers prefer
What changes are required to our Customer Experience to add $1 m (£550,000) in additional revenues?	Determine your Emotional Signature and then run Signature Scenarios to see the financial effect of improving your Emotional Signature in various ways
How can we improve? We are already market leaders but we are not complacent – we want to stay that way	Compare the Emotional Signature of your Promoters and your Detractors
What should we do to convert our Passives to Promoters? Our Net Promoter® Score is high but we have relatively few Promoters and Detractors and a large number of Passives	Compare the Emotional Signature of Passives with that of Promoters

now have tools available to them to address the most elusive part of the Customer Experience, the emotional half. This is a powerful relationship for any Customer Experience proponent to use to answer key questions such as "What do we need to focus on to improve our NPS" or "What changes are required to our Customer Experience to add $1 m (£550,000) in additional revenues?" and so on. Table 8.1 outlines some typical questions we have received from clients, and our responses.

The following case study shows how appreciation of the Emotional Signature and NPS kept the Customer Experience program focused, relevant and sharp.

Case study: Memorial Hermann Hospital System (MHHS)

MHHS is a major regional hospital system with a national reputation and over 15 large hospital facilities. Karen Haney, system executive in charge of Customer Experience, and Rhonda Dishongh, director of customer care, have long been proponents of the Customer Experience. They were fortunate enough to have the support of David Bradshaw, chief information, planning and marketing officer, a no-nonsense but visionary leader. We have been engaged with them for over a year. I worked with them to revamp several of their service lines (treatment areas like cancer, heart and vascular, and so on) and took them through our Moment Mapping® training regimen to accredit them to design emotionally engaging experiences throughout the system.

MHHS had run into the customer satisfaction quandary. Their customer satisfaction scores were high and had improved in the services lines we had worked on. However, they needed more complete information on areas needing further improvement. Karen and Rhonda saw that the Emotional Signature could provide them with a view of how well they were dealing with customers' emotional experience. Once more, David backed them on this. In previous bespoke research we had conducted as part of the Moment Mapping, we learned that their customers (patients and their family or other close caregivers) believed that emotional well-being is responsible for almost a third of their long-term clinical outcome and a third of a hospital's service focus should be on the emotional well-being of customers (Figure 8.6).

Karen and Rhonda wanted to assess the Emotional Signature of MHHS (Figure 8.7). They expected their assessment to be relatively healthy as they had spent the past year working on the complete experience in targeted service lines. They understood the age effect and knew that their inpatient customer base was older (early fifties) compared to the hospital sector (average age early thirties) and so knew that they could expect to see a relatively highly ranked Emotional Signature.

Customers' view of the relative importance of 4 key factors

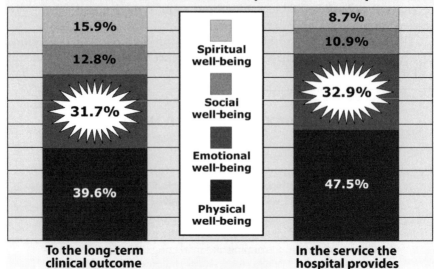

Figure 8.6 The importance of emotional well-being

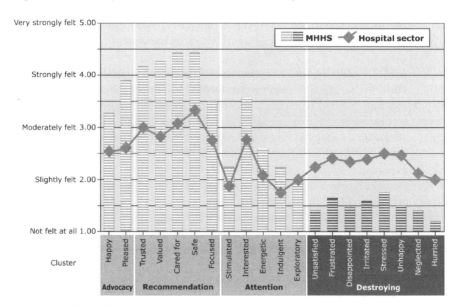

Figure 8.7 MHHS vs hospital sector

On the whole, their Emotional Signature was exceptional. They outperformed their sector almost across the board. None of this was surprising to Karen and Rhonda, having seen the success of patient experience programs in their increased satisfaction scores. In 2003, 87% of their patients said they were satisfied (the same as the national benchmark average). By 2005, 90% of their patients were satisfied compared to a national benchmark average of only 88%. The insight came as we analyzed the cluster scores.

While strong across the board when compared to the sector, MHHS was weakest in the Attention Cluster of emotions (Figure 8.8). The rank order of clusters arranged in terms of strength for MHHS were:

1. Recommendation – 82%
2. Advocacy – 71%
3. Destroying – 71%
4. Attention – 49%.

The better scores for inpatient and outpatient (vs ER (emergency room)) are due to the fact that in the preceding year the Customer Experience program had concentrated on those areas. The ER Customer Experience initiatives were just getting under way.

MHHS is weakest in the Attention Cluster

Average emotion cluster scores*				
	Destroying	Attention	Recommendation	Advocacy
Inpatient	1.48	3.38	4.39	3.78
Outpatient	1.14	2.26	4.26	4.00
ER	1.60	2.07	3.88	3.23
MHHS	1.46	2.47	4.11	3.57

*Note that the Destroying scores are always in a reverse relationship. That is, it is better if the Destroying score is closer to zero, whereas it is better if the Attention, Recommendation and Advocacy scores are closer to 5

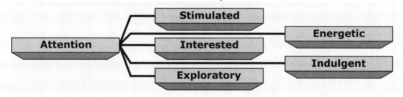

Figure 8.8 Average emotion cluster scores

Indulgent in a hospital?

It may be difficult to see at first glance what the attention emotions (indulgent, stimulated, interested, energetic and exploratory) mean in a hospital setting. Imagine waiting in a traditional waiting room in your average hospital. I think of the boredom and monotony of looking at that goldfish tank, reading the endless magazines on topics of no consequence, or the drone of the TV. Now imagine a waiting room experience that has been designed to be stimulated, indulgent, exploratory and interested. I see learning stations where I can learn about the procedure I am about to undergo, for instance, or personal media players similar to those you find on international air flights where you have a choice of what to look at.

Or consider this, cancer patients who require radiotherapy receive their treatment in a reinforced concrete bunker that is often referred to as a "vault." The patient must lie still in this room while the hum of the machine keeps them company. Even though each session is relatively short, it leaves the patient with nothing to think about except the hum of the machine delivering that dose of radiation. Well, what if the vault experience were designed to drive the attention emotions; there could be a laser light show happening to music selected by the patient while receiving treatment. This vault light show actually exists. The patient not only gets to choose the type of music but the content of the light show (for example cars, golf, ballet, football, and so on). The point is that the Attention emotions in the hospital setting keep us engaged and aware. They keep our minds on positive thoughts and away from idle thoughts that can easily turn negative in a hospital setting.

MHHS were considering using NPS and wanted a reading as to their current NPS. Based on the profile above, the best possible current NPS is estimated to be between 42% and 55%. If they increase their Attention Cluster emotions by an average 5%, they can expect to increase their NPS by about 1%. This would translate into a potential system-wide revenue gain of (let's say) £140.2 m ($255 m). This is not a measly sum under any circumstances but especially for a hospital system that provides upwards of £16.5 m ($30 m) in free care every month to the needy.

With the magnitude of this finding, we compared all the initiatives they were undertaking from the Moment Mapping recommendations and plotted these against the 20 driver and Destroying emotions (Figure 8.9). The purpose of this exercise was to see if and where any gaps existed. This analysis showed that Recommendation was 43% covered, Advocacy was 21% covered, Destroying was 14% covered and Attention was only 11% covered. The initiatives were not doing enough to address the Attention emotions. This area of emotions is being addressed. The Emotional Signature was thus used as a check to keep effective focus on the Customer Experience program.

		Initiative						
		1	2	3	4	5	6	7
Advocacy	Happy							
	Pleased			●		●		●
Recommendation	Trusted	●			●			●
	Valued	●	●	●	●			
	Cared for	●	●			●		●
	Safe					●		●
	Focused		●	●				
Attention	Stimulated							
	Interested		●	●				
	Energetic							
	Indulgent			●				
	Exploratory				●			
Destroying	Unsatisfied					●		
	Frustrated						●	
	Disappointed			●				●
	Irritated						●	
	Stressed							●
	Unhappy							
	Neglected			●				
	Hurried						●	

Figure 8.9 Linking Customer Experience initiatives to the drivers/Destroying

Eureka!

The "eureka" moment here is that I have outlined a method for you to quantify the financial benefits of addressing the emotional side of the Customer Experience; a first and it's a "biggie." This link to financial performance is beneficial, if not crucial, in making the case for the development of an organization's capacity to deliver a consistent, deliberate and complete (that is, physical and emotional) Customer Experience.

Business leaders are "getting it"; an improved Customer Experience leads to sustainable and increased revenues due to a loyal and growing "Promoter" customer base. The fact that CEOs are driving the adoption of NPS at their firms is indication of the momentum that Customer Experience is gaining in the boardroom. However, there are still some Customer Experience Neanderthals lurking about in the corridors, and even a few in corner offices. Most are evolving, but a few resist the inevitable move into the new competitive battleground of the Customer Experience. The ability to model revenue gains based on the emotional engagement with customers can be used to help generate a few more "eureka" moments around the organization and accelerate the evolution of some of these Neanderthals.

Facts do not cease to exist because they are ignored (Aldous Huxley)

Strong reasons make strong actions (William Shakespeare)

As Qaalfa says, how do we deal with these Neanderthals? As we outlined in Chapter 1, how do we convince them that this isn't a religion, but is instead a business imperative? How do we convince our colleagues and bosses that the Customer Experience is worthy of investment in time and resources?

My personal background was working in blue-chip companies, as it was for a number of the Beyond Philosophy team. We have witnessed this resistance at first hand. We understand the politics that drive organizations and we know how to get things done. In fact, we named the company Beyond Philosophy as our belief is that it is OK having a philosophy but you have to go beyond that philosophy and do something! With our experience in strategy and implementation, in the next chapter we tell you about some of the tactics you can use to convince your senior executive this is worth investing in.

Notes

1. Brand extension is the use of a successful brand name to launch a new or modified product in some broad category. For example a kitchen cleaner brand extended as a washing powder brand too. Brand stretching is the use of a successful brand name for goods or services in unrelated markets. For example a well-known motorbike brand that also sells hi-fi, electronics and pianos.
2. "Why Satisfied Customers Defect," T. O. Jones and W. E. Sasser (1995) *Harvard Business Review*.
3. "The One Number You Need to Grow," F. Reichheld (2003) *Harvard Business Review*, December; *The Ultimate Question: Driving Good Profits and True Growth*, F. Reichheld (2006) Harvard Business School Press.
4. *Advocacy Drives Growth: Customer Advocacy Drives UK Business Growth*, P. Marsden, A. Samson and N. Upton (2005) London School of Economics, September.
5. Note that these are not Promoter and Detractor percentages and cannot be used to calculate the NPS. These percentages represent the strength of the emotion scores in the cluster. The higher the percentage, the better the average cluster emotion scores.

9 How to Get Things Done

Before I started Beyond Philosophy, I had spent all my working life in blue-chip companies. This has given me great insight to how things are really done in business. I remember a meeting I attended when working for one of the world's largest telecommunications companies. At the time I was running global customer service for B2B customers, with over 3,500 people reporting to me. It was a monthly "top team" meeting. The team comprised mixed functions, sales, marketing, customer service, HR, and finance. Typically, we spent 80% of the time talking about sales figures, 15% of the time talking about the marketing programs that would get the sales figures, and, oh yes, there was customer service, which got about 5% of the airtime. As you can tell, it was very much a sales culture.

This meeting was unusual as I had a two-hour slot to present my thoughts on customer loyalty. I had prepared well and was looking for commitment to help increase our customer loyalty by redesigning our experiences. After a good debate, everyone agreed customer loyalty was vital and my recommendations were approved. I was encouraged with the outcome as, surprisingly, everyone seemed very positive. I sat back in my chair with a sense of satisfaction. Perhaps this time they meant it, I pondered.

During one of the sales reports on achievement against target, I decided to put this new-found commitment to the customer to the test. I wanted to challenge a fundamental behavior I had always thought was wrong as it created dissatisfied customers as opposed to loyal ones. The subject was bill optimization. In the telecoms industry this is vital. Bill optimization is whether you decide to *proactively* optimize a customer's bill when a new tariff is launched.

The normal practice was that the customer would be informed of a new tariff in some obscure letter that no one read and thus the majority of customers did not change tariff as they did not realize it was available or did not understand how it would benefit them. Up to this point, a bill would only be optimized if a customer contacted us and asked for the new tariff or, as happened increasingly frequently, customers would be approached by a competitor who would offer a better deal if they moved their calls to them. As the incumbent supplier, we would be asked if we could match the offer, or we would pick up the fact the customer wanted to change supplier when they put in the paperwork to change the lines and so on.

Inevitably, as the bills hadn't been optimized for some time, it was easy pickings for the competition as these older prices were not competitive. This also meant we could always go back to the client with a more competitive tariff than their current one. However, here was the problem. It wouldn't take long for the customer to say, "If you could have given me this new tariff for the past 10 months, why have you been allowing me to pay a higher price?" A very good question!

The answer: every time the sales team optimized a customer's bill, they lost revenue, which made it more difficult to achieve their targets. As they were paid 40% of their salary on bonus, against target, the sales teams didn't want to optimize customers' bills. Granted this was a very short-term view and they knew the company would probably lose more in the medium term than they would in the short term, but this is not the way the company drove them. They were judged on whether they achieved their target that month, that quarter, that year. Next year was a long way away and as people changed accounts so regularly, they probably wouldn't have this customer next year, so who cares? Certainly not the senior management team. They would not admit publicly this went on, but everyone knew. It was one of those unspoken truths, a taboo subject that no one talked about as everyone wanted to achieve their targets.

I suggested that as we were now committed to building loyal customers, we should proactively approach customers and tell them we had some great news that could save them money. Yes, I knew this may cost us money in the short term but in the medium and long term it would pay back countless times. You could have heard a pin drop! After a long "debate" where I was in a minority of one, my idea was rejected. I was incensed by the hypocrisy. I complained vociferously that this was wrong, both from a business sense and from a moral sense. I pointed out that on the one hand we talked about the value of loyal customers, and on the other they talked about not optimizing their bills. Nevertheless, it was ignored.

In hindsight, I was probably most disappointed with my boss who sat there and didn't say anything. He also had a vested interest in achieving his target. It was clear that when push came to shove it was OK talking about loyal customers but what really mattered was achieving their target and receiving their bonus at the end of the year. Customer loyalty was a "nice to have." This was another indication to me that I was in the wrong organization.

To ensure that your Customer Experience program is successful it is important that you understand the key motivators of the senior executives.

This story of my experience is typical of many organizations. Sadly, this kind of short-termism is killing business today. It is no surprise that this action results in a poor Customer Experience. The pressure on people to achieve financial targets is increasing year on year and is driving behaviors such as these.

This short-term behavior further builds customer resentment, which shows through in customer churn. In the UK utilities, markets have opened up and the customers who have been treated badly by organizations for years suddenly release their pent-up feelings of resentment against these old monopolies and can't wait to change supplier. These organizations face a massive churn. Reichheld observes:

Right now churn rates in many industries – cellular phones, credit cards, newspapers and cable TV – have deteriorated to the point where a typical company loses half of its new customers in less than 3 years.

AOL's monthly customer churn rate rose to 6% (an annual rate of 72%!).[1]

All because when they had the customers at the beginning, they didn't care. I use the word "care" advisedly, as caring is what it is about.

In today's environment, the pressure to hit numbers increases everyday and "gaming" (to hit your numbers without really hitting your numbers) can frequently take place. In our first book, we talked about the tricks that people in organizations use to achieve their targets, which then affect the Customer Experience. Examples of this are harassing customers to bring forward sales from next year into this year by offering discounts, "mortgaging your business" if you have achieved your targets, keeping orders in your bag for the following year and delaying the order. Given these new circumstances, what are the responses of most organizations? They carry on doing the same as they have done for years only faster and more aggressively, and never mind the customer!

We see short-termism as a disease that is rampant throughout business. It is important that this is understood as it is destroying long-term value in organizations. We have to understand that the CEO will need to be reporting to the city on their progress. Certainly, in my days as a senior executive I was quite often told "We have got to show results to the analysts otherwise they will kill us." This resulted in an increased pressure on senior executives and the management team to perform and produce short-term results which can then lead to the following:

> I was talking to a multinational client. They said their company works on quarterly cycles. At the beginning of the month, everything is laid back and OK, then it starts to ramp up and everyone is trying to get in the sales numbers for the end of the quarter. They had conditioned their customer base so much so that astute customers would wait for the end of the quarter to place their orders as they knew this was the best time to get a good discount as the sales teams struggled to achieve targets. This is a practice common in car dealerships. People know to buy a car at the end of the month, quarter or year for the best discounts.

A definition of madness is doing the same things repeatedly and expecting a different result. Simon Fox, MD of Comet, decided to make a complete change in their reward mechanism as he saw that a focus on commission could cause a poor experience. Simon explains further.

> As part of our Customer Experience program we changed our whole reward scheme as we felt it wasn't driving the experience that we required. We therefore introduced systems that rewarded people for the experience we were trying to deliver. That was a huge exercise with every sales colleague moving away from individual commission. We put a massive investment into training to ensure people "trusted" the knowledge of our staff in the store. We also trained them on "the deliberate journey."

Unfortunately, not every CEO or MD is like Simon. To change the behaviors in your organization, you need to change how people are measured and paid. Getting a percentage of the pay or bonus for achieving targets changed to performance on customer satisfaction, Emotional Signature and Net Promoter® Score (NPS) is a very good start to get people's attention. We have seen only a few organizations that are prepared to change the commission and bonus scheme totally in the first year and therefore you will need to judge the political climate to see what is possible. If a total change is not possible, start off with a smaller percentage, maybe 10–20%, and then over the next couple of years increase this. This is a more pragmatic method.

When talking to senior teams in many multinational blue-chip companies, the pattern of conversation is remarkably similar. When we first engage with clients, it appears there are two types of organization:

1. Those that know they have a problem
2. Those that see this as an opportunity.

The critical first step in implementing a program is to get the senior team committed to this. To do this, it is imperative they understand what you mean by Customer Experience. Some will think you are talking about customer service, some will say they understand, but don't really. Mark Gater, Customer Experience progam manager, who has been leading the implementation at Britannia Building Society, shares his experience with us:

> I think there are some things that are obvious for any program. You've got to have commitment from the top, they really have to understand and buy into it because without that it would just be hopeless. I remember in the beginning we had conversations with the group executive around "what is this Customer Experience concept all about, what does it mean?" Everybody thought it sounded the right thing to do and a really good idea, but they weren't 100% sure what it was.
>
> We created a project that ran for six months which looked at what the Customer Experience is really about. I was concerned that everyone on the senior team understood different things by the phrase "Customer Experience." In fact I now go to Customer Experience conferences and when I find out it's actually about customer service, just with an "experience" label on it, I realize how far our understanding has advanced.

In our view it is vital to go through a stage of what we call "getting it." Getting what the Customer Experience is really about, making sure that people are all looking at this from the same angle. Ensuring people really understand that emotions count for 50% of the Customer Experience and therefore truly appreciate the significance of the Customer Experience. They need to understand the challenges, the changes that will be needed and establish a common language. Neville Richardson, CEO of Britannia Building Society, now looking back on the beginning of their program, reinforces the need for "getting it":

> There was definitely a phrase "getting it" at the beginning. Helping people understand the Customer Experience and gaining involvement, commitment and engagement from

them is important. I particularly remember the session you presented at the Mandarin Oriental Hotel. In the morning we had been on "safari," mystery shopping, around different stores. I was asked to go into a jeweler and ask for a type of watch they didn't sell. I remember being told by the assistant, in a fairly disinterested way, they didn't have it but I should try across the road. This exposure got my commitment incredibly quickly, by putting myself in the customer's shoes and feeling the emotions of a day-to-day interaction. Those two days were absolutely critical to me in furthering my understanding.

We always spend time with the senior teams ensuring they "get it" from the very beginning. We believe this is best achieved through "experiential learning," that is, giving people live Customer Experiences. Therefore we take people on "safari" to give them a real experience. As Neville said, this involves visiting a number of different experiences to see what the Customer Experience is actually like. In our view it is important that people can actually *feel* this experience and subsequent emotions in order to understand the DNA of the Customer Experience. This is very effective for getting people on board. It is critical to ensure that they understand what they will need to do later in the program. Neville Richardson again:

> One of the things we did right at the start of this work was to realize this was an incredibly big and scary program. I think if all we wanted to do was to improve the experience of the customers, we would have done lots of little things that are not necessarily connected. What we wanted to do was create an emotionally engaging Customer Experience and I think the two are different. A deliberate customer experience is something bigger.
>
> I would say be careful of going headlong for a quick win. Everybody wants a quick win, including the board. The danger is this pressure can lead to a false dawn. You could do something to improve the customer service and call it Customer Experience and claim a quick win but in reality you haven't added to the overall experience.

Again, sound advice from Neville. For us this doesn't mean there are no quick wins, but you need to be careful about what you label Customer Experience, otherwise it will just add to the misunderstanding.

Those organizations who know they have a problem with their Customer Experience usually have a good idea of where their problems lie, however, they decide for one reason or another, consciously or subconsciously, not to address this.

When we are engaged by an organization, we typically talk to people who are already committed to improving their experience. Probably people like you, people who are taking the time and trouble to educate themselves further on what they can do to improve their organization's Customer Experience. However, the challenge they face is how to involve their colleagues, the CEO and the board in this thinking and gain their commitment. This can be a difficult task and needs some thought before being attempted, as you normally only have one chance. Therefore it is critical to understand where the senior execs are coming from, and what some of their key drivers are. Let us, then, share some of our insight with you. We have analyzed where the Customer Experience initiatives fail and found it is typically for one of the following two reasons. We also suggest what you could do.

1.
Senior executives don't realize they have a problem with their Customer Experience

It is a constant surprise to us how out of touch a number of senior executives are with their Customer Experience. Too many do not spend any time talking with customers, visiting the front line, or testing their experience. Therefore, to get some engagement, you have to find ways of bringing the reality to them. For instance, talk through the customer satisfaction surveys and ensure they see and understand the results. Arrange for them to spend time with customers, ensure they read customer complaints, and ideally deal with some themselves. Get them to talk with frontline employees who experience the problems every day. Conduct a "mirror" as we have described in previous chapters, tape and video your experience and replay this to them. Employ an external consultant to audit or review your Customer Experience. We get used to telling clients that "your baby is ugly!" Sometimes it is easier and more acceptable if someone from outside the organization delivers a hard message as a wake-up call. This is all comparatively easy.

2.
Senior executives don't really think improving the Customer Experience is important

This is the killer. In our experience, in the beginning most of these people will say that the Customer Experience is important. However, as time progresses, you will often find that they cancel meetings as "something more important has come up." These are the people who don't want to look like they are anti-customers and for political reasons nod their heads and say yes but really mean no.

In our experience, this lack of support can be because they think they understand what the Customer Experience is about, but they don't really, which would indicate they have not been educated well enough. The senior team invariably won't admit this as they don't want to look stupid and admit that they don't understand.

Therefore, the first job is to make sure that everyone understands what is required. Again, in our experience, once they have definitely understood, you will have a number of supporters and a number of people who will agree that something needs to happen, until of course you ask them to do something! They will nod and agree this is fundamentally important. On the surface, they are supportive but actions speak louder than the words.

Therefore, the key question becomes: What can you do to engage them? What will make them do something? Well, in our view, it is simple. You need to ensure that what you are doing is attractive to them. What are their targets? How are they driven, how are they judged? How can we turn this from being a "religion" to something that is just good business sense? What are the senior executives' motivators?

Imagine for one moment that it was decided to pay the senior execs of your organization 100% of their bonus based on customer satisfaction results. Do you think there would be a change in what people do? Of course there would. It would dramatically change their behavior.

The answer is simple; to get engagement we need to make the Customer Experience important to them. If it is important to them, it moves from being a religion to something tangible and measurable. One way of achieving this is to change the measures of management.

Simon Fox, MD Comet, says:

> I had hoped that people would simply embrace the Customer Experience concept and understand the importance of what we were doing. But as we all know it is difficult to change people's behavior. So to keep it alive, you need to measure it regularly. I think without doing this it could have been just like many other initiatives that never took hold.

Measurement is vital and this is where a number of organizations now use the NPS and Emotional Signature to achieve this.

Many things motivate people. But pain is a great motivator! Ask yourself what typically causes CEOs pain?

- Not achieving the profitability targets
- Not hitting budget
- Not achieving their headcount targets
- A poor share price.

These are the big ones. Where does this pain come from?

- The chairman
- City analysts
- Shareholders
- The media
- A regulator.

If they achieve these objectives, what do they get?

- Bonus
- Job retention
- Future job prospects

■ Building their reputation
■ Job satisfaction.

Let's go back to my budget airline experience in Chapter 1 – an appalling experience where they couldn't care less. Here is an actual headline from the BBC news that appeared about this airline, the name being changed for anonymity:

> Company "AAE" has said that better sales will boost its 2006 profits by as much as 50%, an increase on its previous projection of 10% to a 15% rise.

Do you think they are doing a good job? On the face of it, yes, I am sure the execs are happy. Now imagine you are trying to convince these execs that they need to change. Why would they? You can imagine everyone looking around and saying, "The world looks pretty good to me, why change? Why suffer the pain of change?"

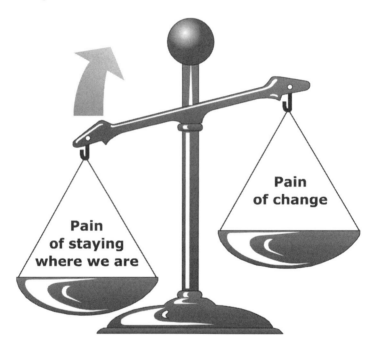

Figure 9.1 Balancing the pain

It's a good question. The answer is that these numbers could be much better if they improved the Customer Experience. To illustrate this to them we need to prove a business case and then shift the balance between the pain of staying where they are today and the pain of change (Figure 9.1). It is important, therefore, that you realize:

The PERCEIVED pain of change has to be less than the pain of staying where they are

To get the senior executives of any organization to change, they need to be motivated to do so. At the moment too many don't see that improving the Customer Experience will help them achieve their goals, and therefore they are not fully engaged despite the rhetoric of "wanting to be customer focused." They have recognized that they have a series of targets to achieve, primarily financial. Their experience and success in their careers have shown them they can achieve their targets by slashing budgets and providing incentives for the salesforce to sell more. They can change the commission structure even if it does "mortgage" business. Being good at these things has got them where they are today, so why change? Why do something they don't understand? You can't blame them.

Therefore, the senior executives need to see how the Customer Experience can help them achieve their revenue target and save them costs. They need to be shown an alternative to the short-termism that is driving behaviors which are ironically destroying value in the Customer Experience. For example, when you slash your budgets to achieve your headcount target, this can mean that you don't have enough people answering the phone, customers are kept waiting longer which evokes "frustrated" and "disappointed," emotions from the Destroying Cluster. You can now show them how this is costing them money. When you look into the DNA of the Customer Experience, you see that this short-term action evokes more of the destroying emotions and you can explain how it will be more difficult to hit next year's target. They are cutting off their nose to spite their face.

Your role is to get them to see the light. Hopefully we have demonstrated how we have converted a religion into a tangible business asset. You will now be able to demonstrate to your senior executives how others have improved their Customer Experience and have a tangible business benefit that will help them achieve their targets. We hope this book will give you the financial examples that you will be able to use with your senior execs and get the change that is needed.

Finally, at one of our last public education events, we asked the group of 35 people to list down, in their experience, why projects succeed and why they fail. We hope this will act as a decent checklist for your project. This is by no means a comprehensive list and we are sure that any decent project management book would list additional items, but this is from people who have actually been doing the work. Clearly, a number of the reasons for success are also the reasons for failure, if not addressed.

Table 9.1 Why Customer Experience projects succeed and fail

Why projects succeed	Why projects fail
Have senior management support	No support from the top
People on the project believe in what you are trying to do	People don't really believe
Strong leadership all around	Lack of leadership
Strong project management	Weak project management
Project involving the right mix of people – levels, functions, experience	All the team is from one area of the business. Silo approach
Teamwork all around	Team members have different agendas and conflicts
Project team are prepared to take risks	Project team not prepared to take risks
Challenges the norm	Sticks with what they do now
Clear scope	Unclear scope
Clear objective	Unclear objective
Clear responsibilities	Unclear responsibilities
Clear business benefit	No business need
Adequate resources and budget allocated	Not enough resources and resource conflict
Produces tangible results	Intangible results – no measurement
Senior champion for the project	Poor role modeling by senior people
Project tied to the strategic goals of the company	Project not tied to strategic goals
Shared understanding of the goals	No shared understanding of goals
Produces quick wins	Always promising tangible benefits but not delivering
Uses current systems – not having to replace them	Proposes a massive system change
Good consistent communications	Poor or no communications
Varied communications	Too much reliance on one communication channel
Realistic measures	Unrealistic measures
Time spent building strategy that has buy-in	No time spent on strategy, straight into action
"Getting it" for all levels of people	Not enough people "getting it"
Change management	No change management
Employee engagement	Lack of representatives from around the business
Clear decision making	No clear decision making
Empowerment	No empowerment of project team
Stakeholder management	No stakeholder management
Project plan with clear milestones	Unrealistic time scales and deadlines
External perspective	Too internally focused, no external perspective
Customer testing – piloting	No customer testing or involvement
Good customer research	No customer research – "we know what customers want" attitude

In this chapter we have been talking about how to get senior execs motivated for this change. As you have read throughout this book, there are a growing number of organizations with senior execs who have been working on this for some time. TNT is one of them and it provides a great case study, demonstrating the effects that this work can bring. Let's read about this in the next chapter.

Note

1. *The Ultimate Question: Driving Good Profits and True Growth*, F. Reichheld (2006) Harvard Business School Press.

10 Show Me the Money – TNT Case Study

Imagine you have been working late for the past week to ensure an important bid is submitted to a client on time. This deal is worth 30% of your target. You have been working night and day on this and as a consequence you haven't seen your family very much. In fact your partner is now in a bad mood with you as you have missed a couple of important family events. Today is the day the bid needs to be in. Thank goodness, you have just finished on time. However, the tender document states you must get a hard copy to them. The problem is that the customer is over 200 miles away! You decide to send it by a courier who can deliver it on the same day.

What mood are you in when you call the courier? *Stressed*, worried, anxious, *hurried*. When you get through to their sales office, you are treated like a transaction. They do not pick up on your stressed state and do nothing to put you at your ease; they simply take your details and say someone will be around to pick up the document. You put the phone down and now you're even more stressed! Why? They have not instilled a sense of confidence in you that your document will be delivered on time, as you felt they seemed to deal with you in a blasé manner. It may be an everyday occurrence to them but not for you. "Don't they realize how important this is?" you ask yourself. As you are feeling this way, you phone them on four separate occasions to see if the document has been delivered. Their website is confusing and you want human contact and the reassurance this brings. The irony is, this imposes a cost on the courier company and wastes your time, making you a dissatisfied customer. You certainly don't feel *valued* or *cared for,* and it's definitely not making you *happy*.

This can be a typical interaction with any number of courier companies in a highly competitive market. On the face of it, it's a simple transaction, but when you start to look into what they do, it can be a very emotional engagement with their wide and varied customer base. Quite an interesting industry to work in.

I first met Bob Black at the launch of our first book *Building Great Customer Experiences* in 2002. We had decided to hold the global launch at the BT Tower, which provides great views over central London.

Bob is now the chief operating officer of TNT Express Services in the UK. TNT Express Services is the leading B2B express delivery company in the UK with an annual revenue in excess of £850 m ($1,530 m) and employs 10,600 people. They have a fleet of 3,500 vehicles operating out of more than 70 locations. The UK business is the largest business unit in the TNT

Express global network, which has a presence in 63 countries and delivers to more than 200 nations.

The UK business delivers over 50 million items each year on behalf of tens of thousands of customers. Globally, TNT Express employs 48,000 people with revenue of €5.3 billion (£4 billion approx, $6.5 billion approx) in 2005. This is a huge, highly logistical organization and by necessity is physically based. Not one that you would normally associate with focusing on an emotional Customer Experience. Hence we thought it would make a great case study.

I have always found Bob to be practical, a down-to-earth leader who naturally commands great respect from his people. He has been promoted through the ranks of TNT and demonstrates a gift for strategic thinking, but then has the rare gift of breaking the actions down into a clear and simple action plan. Since our first meeting at BT Tower we have been pleased to work with Bob at different stages of his journey to improve TNT's Customer Experience.

Bob was one of the clients who, rightly so, asked us to quantify the returns of the work on the Customer Experience. Intuitively Bob knew this was the right thing to do, but he wanted to understand the financial return the actions would give. It was the influence of Bob and other clients that drove us to develop the Emotional Signature of Value, and thus this book, so it seems appropriate that we report back on TNT's considerable progress.

I will let Bob pick up the story.

Bob: TNT was started in 1946 in Australia. In those early years, the company offered a five-day delivery service, however, by the 1970s, a "next day" delivery was common across that huge continent. In the UK, in the late 1970s, TNT acquired Inter County Express. TNT recognized the need to improve service delivery, recognizing that a five-day delivery service was clearly quite backward considering the size of the UK when compared to Australia.

The result was the launch of a three-day delivery service entitled Tristar. Not content with that level of service improvement, TNT became the first company to offer a guaranteed next-day delivery proposition for its UK customers in the early 1980s. As a recognized innovative force in the express delivery sector, groundbreaking and pioneering initiatives became synonymous with the TNT name.

In the early 1990s we were market leaders and our brand was very strong. When I look back now, you could say we were quite arrogant. We had little competition and thus our margins were good. Maybe we became a little complacent. We thought no one could establish the type of infrastructure needed as quickly as we had, or at least if anyone started we would see them and would then be able to react. However, business has a strange habit of biting you when you least expect it, especially if you get complacent. Before we knew it we were hit with a new concept from left field; a franchise type of operation that used single operators working out of different towns or cities. These really caused us a lot of pain. They became stronger in their technology, infrastructure and their own trunking capabilities but fortunately they couldn't reach the heights of the services which we were providing.

This spurred us into action and we started to review our rates and innovate again. We introduced a set rate contract for a 12-month period. This was well received by our customers as it gave them a stable fee structure; again this gave us the edge, but only for a while. In hindsight, we have always focused on improving the "physical" aspects of the experience as we hadn't even thought about the emotional side at that stage. We did notice that it was very easy for our competition to copy us. We were finding the time from "innovation to imitation" seemed to be getting shorter and shorter.

In 2000 we saw the opportunity to establish a whole new business of value-added services that looked at managing the mail rooms of companies and other parts of their supply chain, called TNT Express Specialist Services (TESS). I took on my current role to do this. A major part of this organization consisted of some very mature products like "Sameday" which is our same-day delivery service that had been around since the early 1980s. Other parts of the business were very new and exciting in the marketplace.

Although the competition had improved, they hadn't quite caught us up. We realized our lead wouldn't last long if we didn't act soon. In 2001–2002, in TESS, we undertook a large customer survey to provide us with a real in-depth understanding of the business. We discovered we were not engaging as well with the customers as we had done previously.

We discovered, in essence, our customers were saying you're good, you're still the market leader, you're doing a good job, but you don't answer your phones quickly enough, sometimes we don't feel that you are interested in what we are doing, you're a bit process driven and your people can be too structured and robotic. When I look back, we were starting to drive the destroying cluster of emotions you are talking about in this book. Therefore, in early 2003 we started discussions with you at Beyond Philosophy about how we could improve our experience. You made us look at the world from a different angle, not just from the physical side but from an emotional angle. To help us understand this further, we asked you to undertake further research, visiting our depots and talking with our customers to get a sense as to what was going on, to understand the emotional context of how they were feeling, as our survey was, on reflection, quite physically driven.

The results of this work really opened our eyes and set us on our way to fundamentally change the business. We now realized that our customers were right, we were too process driven, too transactional in our approach to them. We discovered that for many customers this was quite an emotional experience and that we had not recognized this before.

Colin: If I can just take you back for a moment. It's quite interesting that we are talking about customer feelings as if it's quite natural. However, I remember in the beginning running a couple of sessions for your senior management team and talking about customer emotions for the first time. This is not normal business language, is it? What was it that made you intuitively feel this was the right thing to do?'

Bob: I guess I had always considered that service was a key to success but had not really made this strong emotional link, until you pointed it out. I believe this is now fundamentally important. My view is this must be believed in by people, it's got to be invested in, so people start seeing and believing it's the right thing to do. Once we'd taken the decision, this was the next big battleground we needed to conquer – it required focus. The good news was, the management team had bought in so we were all aligned to move forward.

Colin: What would you say was the most common objection you had to overcome when you started down this path?

Bob: The first questions are usually, Where's the value in it? Will this really change anything? What's in it for us? These are the common objections. People also say Why should we change? What does this mean to me? Why do I need to change? What are we doing wrong now? These were the tough ones. My management team asked about the financial benefit. There was a concern this would just be "flavor of the month." In my view, it is important to put some consistency behind this kind of initiative and ensure the management team is supportive from the beginning. We did have one manager who didn't buy in. He was causing us a problem with the team below him. After a lot of time spent trying to convince and coach him, it was obvious it wasn't working, and therefore I had to remove him because he didn't believe in it, he didn't see it as important. This also sent out a message that I was serious.

Colin: You also took our advice and created a Customer Experience Statement, which you called a Customer Charter. Tell me about that.

Bob: Our work with you revealed we needed to define the experience we were trying to deliver. To do this I took my management team away for two days and we put together the Customer Charter based on customer research. We very much focused on the key emotional things: empathy, trust and understanding. As they were formulated by the management team they felt ownership of them. We talked about it and discussed what the differentials would be, we reviewed our competitors, what were they doing, were they doing different things or not? What weren't they doing that we could do better, and so on? This is not a decision that should be taken half-heartedly. My view is either do it or don't do it. I think there is nothing worse than confusing your own employees on what you want to achieve.

It is important everyone sees this as being part of the culture and not just flavor of the month. You need to be serious about it. For example, to demonstrate our commitment we have appointed a general manager of Customer Experience and a director of Customer Experience. In my view you need to be clear this is a cultural change, it isn't an instant change, it's a journey and it's never complete because customer expectations continue to rise, and so it will go on forever.

Colin: But why focus on the Customer Experience? Why bother?

Bob: We could see from our statistics that we are in a mature market, and to grow we needed to gain market share from our competitors. We felt the Customer Experience was the best way to do this. It was obvious to me that we could no longer focus just on price and products. Customers wanted to feel more engaged. The evidence was all very compelling. Our retention of accounts and our growth rate on accounts weren't as high as we would've liked. After some dialog with the management team, and your help in interpreting some of this data, it was clear that we weren't maintaining a good customer contact and we weren't differentiating ourselves. We were churning rather than maintaining, therefore we weren't growing, and it was costing us a lot of money. My view was we didn't have a choice if we want to be market leaders.

Armed with the Customer Charter, the research data and your work, we began to think how we could engage our people. They had been very process driven for a number of years and we wanted them to be more empathetic and understand the emotional requirements of the customer. To help achieve this, in mid-2003 we conducted our national conference themed on the Customer Experience. You will recall you gave a speech. We decided to give the delegates a real experience of how it feels to be a customer of TNT from an emotional perspective. It was therefore a very different type of conference!

To do this we decided to give them as near a real experience as we could. We arranged an enormous game where they needed to book and go on a holiday. The 450 delegates were asked to break into groups, make the travel arrangements, that is, get foreign currency, pick up tickets, travel to the airport, go through customs, get on the flight, fly to the destination, have the holiday, and then fly back. We planned the experiences to give the delegates the same emotions that our customers felt in dealing with us. Therefore people had either a good, bad or indifferent experience. I remember very well the levels of frustration, the stress and anxiety the delegates felt as they navigated the various barriers we put in their way. I remember there were some huge arguments and real discomfort felt among some of the delegates. It made a huge impact on people.

On the other side, we had built some great experiences where people bought foreign currency, went through passport control and enjoyed a VIP lounge. They were drinking champagne and enjoying themselves and were laughing at the people who were having a poor experience!

Colin: How important was it to actually make them experience the barriers and emotions and feel them for themselves?

Bob: It was fundamental. Unless they realize what it really feels like to be a customer it's difficult for some people to imagine. Until people experience those barriers I don't think they ever realize they exist, or at least they make excuses as to why they're there. It was fundamentally important to ensure people knew how our customers were feeling every day.

Colin: Why do you think that you had unwittingly put up barriers to the customer?

Bob: Like many organizations we were very process driven. The good news is, we recognize that now. We had put in place these processes to ensure people didn't slip out of line. But we overplayed our hand. We really want our people to be more natural in the way they talk with customers, and the irony is, that is what they wanted as well. We needed to build a process which allowed them to be natural in their conversation, rather than robotic. We needed to fully understand the customers' emotions, and then empathize with them to make them feel involved in the process.

Colin: How do you now ensure the Customer Experience is being delivered on the front line?

Bob: The reality is that this isn't something you correct overnight and it isn't something you can assume will continually be done. It's a journey, not a destination. Therefore, to keep the focus, we now test our experience through a mystery shopper program. Importantly, we do not just look at the physical aspects of the experience but the emotional side as well. We look at the emotions in the clusters you are discussing in this book. The Sameday delivery can be a very emotional experience, so we now look at the emotional state of the customer coming into the experience, what's the urgency of the delivery? What's driving that urgency? What could be the consequences of non-delivery? Through our work with you we know these are important issues.

We also tape the calls and feedback to the agents on how they are doing, not from a process perspective, but from an emotional one. For instance, you sounded *hurried* when you spoke to the customer and tried to close the conversation down very quickly. What could you do to improve this? The customer was feeling *stressed* so why didn't you take the time to calm them down? The customer was *disappointed* that we couldn't give them the delivery time they wanted, what could we have done differently? It felt like you only had two minutes to do the job, maybe you should slow down.

With your help, we understood that we needed to look at the emotions coming into the experience, some of which we can't control, but they still affect our experience so we have to devise strategies to cope with them.

Colin: What have been the results of this focus on the Customer Experience and emotions?

Bob: In the past three years we have grown the Sameday account base by 50%, which is fantastic. We've doubled our revenue in the five-year period from £80 m to £160 m ($144–288 m); a 100% increase in revenue growth, and a significant part of this is due to the action we have taken on improving our Customer Experience. It is important we are not complacent though, as customer's expectations will grow and we will constantly have to change and refine things.

Colin: If you've increased the customer base by 50%, your churn must have reduced substantially and therefore you must have saved money there as well?

Bob: We believe a lost customer costs us ten times more to regain them, because if they go, they could tell eight to ten people. If they're not happy with us it's tougher to get them back, so every time we lose a customer we have to gain ten new customers to replace them. So yes, we believe this has saved us a substantial amount of money as it has improved our churn.

Colin: That's very impressive and something I am sure you're all proud of. To make this live a bit more, can you give me an example of the types of things you have changed.

Bob: Call backs and complaints handling are a good example. In the past we found our customers said they were *frustrated* or *irritated* as they would call us and would be passed around the organization with no one taking responsibility. Now the person who takes the initial call is the person who is responsible for this customer throughout the process and deals with any complaint. So people are no longer being passed around. We have seen that this has made our customers feel less frustrated. Another example is when customers are feeling *stressed,* we need to be empathetic towards them. This doesn't mean having a 20-minute chat with them, as that could cause them stress as well! It's just about doing the right thing for them, whatever that may be.

Colin: I believe you also made a major change in the way that you marketed to your customers?

Bob: Yes, since the early 1980s we have typically used an "incentives to trade" for the customer. This essentially means giving away gifts such as toy trucks, wind-up radios, coffee mugs, footballs, and so on. This had always worked well for us, however, given we now understand customer requirements in more depth and in light of the new exper-ience we were trying to deliver, we made the brave decision to change this. We felt that the incentives to trade were no longer appropriate and there was a better way to market ourselves. It was a brave decision as incentives to trade was a tried and tested formula which we knew worked, and we had been doing it for years. However, our belief was that if we were going to move on to the next level, then things needed to change and this was one of them. We wanted to emotionally engage with our customers.

    We also decided to run the campaign more frequently, once every six weeks, rather than typically once every six months, with a view to being in front of the customer with something fun. So now, for example, as we know when customers enter our experience they are feeling stressed due to the importance of getting the package delivered, we have mailed them a "stress barometer." Something that is fun, but also gets the message over that we know how they feel. Another example is that we have mailed them bubble wrap, the stuff people love popping, to relieve stress. We have sent crossword puzzles, again to relieve stress and to be stimulating, exploratory, and so on. The irony is that customers love it and it is less expensive than the incentives to trade program! Due to this saving we can afford to be in front of customers more frequently.

Another example is when we sent out the crossword puzzle, we placed the answers on the website to again start an interaction with customers; we gave them a wheel with an arrow and they could write people's names from the office around the edges so they could spin the wheel to find out whose turn it was to make the drinks. We sent them some fake animal fur and indicated in the message that statistics show stroking fur can relieve stress. We sent things like camomile herbal teabags saying, "Are you having a stressful day? Here's a herbal teabag for you; sit down and relax." We sent a lavender scratch card, and then we gave them some information on lavender which has stress-relieving qualities. Some really great ideas and customers love them!

All these ideas came out of our desire to emotionally engage with our customers and evoke the emotions you are now calling the Attention Cluster: *interested*, *stimulated*, *indulgent* and *exploratory*.

The feedback was great and our customers said it was all good fun, but it really gets a serious message in front of them. The TNT experience is about de-stressing them, it's about relaxing. It's not about being uptight, it's not about being stressed, it's not about feeling unwanted. It's about letting them know we care for them.

Colin: And have the conversion rates been any different between this and the incentive to trade approach?

Bob: Yes, there's higher re-trade and higher new trade on all of those. We've seen something like a 20% uptake over and above the "traditional" mailshot.

Colin: For the people who are just starting on the emotional side of the experience, perhaps you could give us your perspective on how the emotions that drive and destroy value affect your business and how you used them.

Bob: We started off by trying to control the emotions that destroy value: *frustrated*, *irritated*, *unsatisfied*, *stressed* and *disappointed*. These are the emotions that we believe really drive up your churn rates and therefore they cost you a lot of money. We spent time investigating what we were doing to evoke these emotions and what we needed to do to change. Some of the things are really easy to fix, some more difficult. The reality is that you'll never totally get rid of these emotions. If the customer rings and the person they're talking to is feeling unhappy, as a flu bug has hit the depot and there are not enough people to answer the phone that day, then the customer is going to be hurried and irritated. But we now try and plan for these eventualities. You'll never eradicate them, but you can minimize them.

154

We also try and make sure that our people don't feel stressed and that they ask for help if they need it. It's management's responsibility to create the right atmosphere to enable the frontline people to perform for the customer.

We then started to look at the emotions that drive value like interested stimulated and focused, which is fundamentally important as you want these to occur at your first point of contact. Do you demonstrate you are interested in your customers and are the customers *interested* in what you can do for them? That is your first positive engagement with them. If you can apply your enthusiasm, then they will feel *energized*. In our experience we can induce a short-term peak by getting customers to feel *interested* and *exploratory* with us and feel *stimulated* with our new marketing approach. All the items that I have described, the lavender, the camomile tea, are all about being interesting and stimulating; the crossword puzzle evokes feelings of exploratory and stimulates customers. Focusing on these emotions, in my view, is a significant reason for the success of these programs.

However, to get customers for life you have to *value* them and thus evoke the Recommendation and Advocacy Clusters of emotions, not just once but every time. It's about knowing who they are, knowing what they want, and then understanding their needs. They will then feel they can *trust* you. They know that you have delivered on your promise and that you *cared for* them and the delivery is *safe* in your hands. All this then ultimately leads to a *happy* customer.

Colin: That's great, a really good application of the emotions. One thing we haven't covered is how TNT employees reacted to all this customer-focused work?

Bob: They much prefer it. Quite obvious in hindsight. Do you prefer inter-action with a customer and helping them, or being stuck to rigid processes? As a result of this and other initiatives, our attrition has reduced from 33% to 20%, which is a substantial decrease. This is fantastic for us in terms of employee engagement. I think actually the employees are enjoying being given more flexibility, having to engage with customers more, but less in process and more in emotional, and enjoying the job more. This, therefore, also means we save money on recruitment and training and have more experienced people out there as well.

It's a huge statement to us. Not only is our engagement with employ-ees greater, but engagement with the customer is greater. We demon-strate the improvements through results, customer growth and revenue growth. The drivers are having a stable workforce and happy customers. What else do you want out of it, to be honest with you? You've got happy customers, you've got a happy workforce and your business results are going in the right direction, its great!

Colin: The whole program has been a tremendous success and the results are really good, I know that everyone at TNT is very proud of their achievements. We look forward to hearing more.

11 Some Good Advice

As this book comes to a close we hope we have converted you to a belief in the emotional side of the Customer Experience and the value this can bring to your organization. We also hope that armed with the four clusters of emotions that drive and destroy value you will be able to make the business case with your organization to improve your experience.

We would like to leave you with some advice from our clients as they are seasoned professionals who have gone through the the pain of implementing a successful Customer Experience program.

When we conducted interviews with these people, we finished each interview with the following two questions. "What advice would you give people who are trying to improve their Customer Experience?" and "What benefits have you seen from this work?"

Chuck Kavitsky (CEO Fireman's Fund Insurance Company)

What should the CEO or leader do? The greatest way of finding the truth is to do some of your own research, start reading letters you send to your customers, phone the call centers, and talk to customers direct. Within a relatively short time of actually getting a first-hand experience of those things, you will find out that what you are hearing about how perfect everything is, is not true.

The strongest advice I think I would give a CEO heading down this path is that he should expect to hear from his people that they're already doing it and they understand it. He should expect to hear if they do more it'll just cost more money and they won't get a return. He should expect to hear from his people that they're very sensitive to these issues. He should understand that when he hears this from his people, his people are not lying to him. The reality is that his people are giving him those answers honestly, and believe what they are saying. But again the reality is that they just don't fully understand and "get it."

I've got a lot of work ahead of me, but I have the kind of work that could change the shape of a company. The first thing you have to do is not get mad or angry at people; it's one of those things where everybody had the right intentions, where everybody thought they knew what they were doing, but it's so easy to get lost. It's easy to get lost because we're already experts and we have the answers. In reality, in this case it's all about asking the right questions.

We do something which we call "able to," "want to," and "allow to." Being "able to" means the person has the knowledge and the skills; "want to" means their compensation, recognition and measurement is in line so that they have a motivation to do it. The last one is "allow to" which is kind of the empowerment. I am trying to get people to think differently so that they feel more empowered and "allowed to" go through the end-to-end process. What I'm trying to teach is a whole different way of thinking, and the problem that people have is that we're taught by school and we're taught by our parents and we're taught by the companies we work at, we're taught the answer first and then somebody introduces the question to which that's the answer. I think the key issue is teaching people to ask the right questions.

Our Net Promoter® Score as a company has been going up. We have moved our position up against what we call our key competition, which is seven companies. We were below the medium, now we're above the medium. We actually went up about 20% which is down to all the work we have been doing to improve the Customer Experience.

It's a journey, and what I don't want to do is give an impression we're there. What I will say is we're heading in the right direction and we clearly have had movement. Our people have great pride in the fact that we're a major contributor to the fire service in terms of grants for equipment, and they have great pride in recognizing the moral aspects and the emotional aspects of what we do. That's a very key issue because once you start to get people's hearts and minds this moves the whole process forward quickly.

Maxine Clark (CEO Build-A-Bear Workshop)

If I was advising another CEO on how to go down this path, the first thing I would say is they have to feel passionate about it. If you're passionate about it, you can give your heart and soul to it. I think the successful brands in the world like the Virgin brand in the UK or Build-A-Bear Workshop, Starbucks, Zara, the people behind those brands really felt there was a need to fill a void and are passionate about the business that they're in.

It has to come from the top of a company; it has to be in that company's DNA. How can the sales associates believe it and make it happen every day if their store manager doesn't feel that way or the company owner doesn't feel that? There is a certain amount that can be accomplished, but you just can't go the full distance unless everybody's on board.

Simon Fox (MD Comet)

They [the CEOs] need to put themselves personally at the front of the program and make sure that it's done very rigorously as I think it could be very easy to underestimate the time and effort this takes in reinforcing the message and making sure things are happening. It needs to be very rigorous and thoughtful.

I would advise anyone to think about their Customer Experience very deeply and make sure that this really is at the center of their strategy. This is something you cannot do lightly. It's something you either do completely or not at all. You have to determine whether it is right for your business. I don't think it is right for everybody, but it is certainly right for our business.

I think the main concern around the business was that they thought this would be a passing fad. Organizations are very good at launching initiatives that are "flavor of the month." Therefore there were a few people who put their heads down and hoped the flavor of the month would pass and they would be able to go straight back to doing what they did before.

Focusing on the Customer Experience has a number of by-products; there is no doubt this has led to a lower cost in recruitment, better productivity, better first time success – so there are concrete business measures. I think that it will take time for them to flow through but there's no question that I am really excited about the results.

Neville Richardson (CEO Britannia Building Society)

What advice would I give to someone starting down this route? Firstly, I would say if people don't understand why you want to put customers first, then don't bother, because I think if it becomes a mechanical process then it doesn't mean anything. I think you've got to capture the emotions of the people that work with you. If you ensure they understand why it's important, they get behind it and then they need to understand why the emotions are important.

I think too many businesses talk about outputs and not about how things are achieved, they talk about what comes out at the end of it and not how they got there. We started looking at the "how" in detail, for example how do you feel walking into a branch?

We're now making management decisions based around the Customer Experience and we're building this into our planning process. When any of the management team are planning a change, they are expected to consider the Customer Experience. One of my roles, when I'm chairing the executive board meeting, is to ask "Have you considered the implications on the Customer Experience?" You don't have to ask questions too often for people to realize this is a standard question and one they had better have thought through!

Our complaints have gone down by 40% over the past two years and our customer satisfaction levels and our customer advocacy levels are the highest they've ever been in this business. We are also delighted to have won the Unisys Customer Service award this year. So a great start, but still a long way to go – these are facts about our perform-ance, but we don't know how much of this is down to what we've done so far on Customer Experience; obviously some will be, but we've only just started the journey.

Some wise words from some great practitioners! We hope you have enjoyed reading this book and that we have provided you with a stimulating and inter-esting Customer Experience. We wish you well, and if you have any questions, observations or feedback you would like to share, please don't hesitate to contact us via our website (beyondphilosophy.com) or email me direct at colin.shaw@ beyondphilosophy.com. To show we value you, we would be happy to answer any questions you may have; also, we are always looking for good stories for the next book! We wish you good luck in building great Customer Experiences.

Index